GOURMET GAME NIGHT

GOURMET GAME NIGHT

bite-sized,
mess-free eating for
board-game parties,
bridge clubs, poker nights,
book groups, and more

BY CYNTHIA NIMS

PHOTOGRAPHY BY SHERI GIBLIN

TEN SPEED PRESS
Berkeley

Copyright © 2010 by Cynthia Nims
Photographs copyright © 2010 by Sheri Giblin

Published in the United States by Ten Speed Press, an imprint
of the Crown Publishing Group, a division of Random House,
Inc., New York.
www.crownpublishing.com
www.tenspeed.com

Ten Speed Press and the Ten Speed Press colophon are regis-
tered trademarks of Random House, Inc.

Library of Congress Cataloging-in-Publication Data
Nims, Cynthia C.
    Gourmet game night : bite-sized, mess-free eating for
board-game parties, bridge clubs, poker nights, book groups,
and more / by Cynthia Nims. — 1st ed.
        p. cm.
    Includes index.
    Summary: "Creative and whole-foods recipes designed
to keep fingers clean during hand-intensive activities such as
board game parties, poker nights, knitting groups, and more"—
Provided by publisher.
1. Appetizers. 2. Entertaining. I. Title.
    TX740.N56 2010
    641.8'12—dc22

                                    2009033779

ISBN 978-1-58008-088-0
Printed in China

Design by Katy Brown
Food styling by Dan Becker
Prop styling by Leigh Noe
Photography assistance by Jen Wainz

10 9 8 7 6 5 4 3 2 1

First Edition

I dedicate this book to the name of fun: to kicking back,
to getting together with friends, to eating and drinking well,
to laughing a lot, and to competing just a bit.

Contents

x Acknowledgments

1 Introduction

3 Getting Game

5 About the Recipes

7 The Essentials

8 Basic Techniques

10 Serving Tips

11 Menu Planning

1 Dips and Spreads

18 Caesar Dip with Big Croutons and Romaine

19 Edamame Purée in Cherry Tomatoes

20 Crostini with Wild Mushroom Tapenade

22 Oven-Baked Potato Chips with Onion Dip

24 Radishes with a Trio of Dips

27 Homemade Pretzel Sticks with Three Mustards

29 Crostini with Chicken Liver Mousse and Kumquats

30 Green Pea and Mint Spread with Crispy Pancetta

32 Individual Cheese Fondues with Apples and Ham

34 Brown Butter Pound Cake with Caramel Dip

36 Personal Chocolate-Port Fondues

❷ Skewers and Picks

39 Pickled Grape and Blue Cheese Skewers

40 Grilled Garlicky Mushrooms

41 Wasabi Pea–Crusted Tuna

42 Pork Saltimbocca

43 Herb-Marinated Shrimp

45 Swordfish and Fennel Skewers

46 Spicy Meatballs with Yogurt-Cucumber Dip

48 Lamb and Olive Kebabs

49 Peppered Steak with Balsamic Red Onions

50 Beef Yakitori

52 Mole Flank Steak with Pickled Peppers

❸ All-Edibles

55 Aged Cheddar with Dried Cherry–Almond Chutney

56 Artichoke-Stuffed Mushrooms

57 Mini Tostadas with Cumin Black Beans

58 Tuna Tartare on Daikon Slices

59 Herbed Biscuits with Smoked Salmon

60 Salmon Poke in Endive Leaves

62 Polenta Squares with Spicy Sausage and Spinach

64 Stuffed Large Pasta Shells with Kale-Ricotta Filling

65 Baby Baja Tacos

66 Shrimp Cakes in Shiso Leaves

68 Roasted Red Potatoes with Bacon-Chive Crème Fraîche

69 Meringues with Fresh Berry Filling

70 Orange Tuile Cones with Cassata Filling

72 Mocha Cheesecake Bars

73 Cinnamon Meringues with Chocolate Mousse

4 Sandwiches

5 Pastries

6 Small Dishes

76 Petits Croque Monsieurs

77 Chicken Salad Sandwiches with Orange and Walnuts

78 Itty Bitty BLTs

80 Pimento Cheese Tower Sandwiches

81 Pork Tenderloin with Rhubarb Chutney

83 Lamb Burgers with Feta

84 Walnut Sablés with Maple-Walnut Cream

86 PB&J Blondie Bites

89 Ice Cream Sandwiches

91 Banana Bread with Hazelnut–Cream Cheese Filling

95 Almost Bite-Sized Pizzas

97 Olive and Cheese Crackers

98 Roasted Fennel Focaccia with Pecorino

100 Beef Empanadas with Black Beans and Jalapeño

102 Mushroom and Goat Cheese Tartlets

103 Empanadas with Chicken and Walnut

105 Chocolate Tartlets with Brandy Cream

106 Nutella and Banana Galettes

108 Raspberry and Cream Cheese Turnovers

110 Cumin Spiced Nuts

111 Sage Popcorn

112 Chilled Avocado Soup with Roasted Poblano Cream

114 Green Gazpacho

115 Lentil and Carrot Soup with Cilantro Purée

116 Celery, Radish, and Parsley Salad with Lemon Dressing

118 Fennel and Corn Salad

119 Baked Clams with Smoked Paprika

121 Curried Coconut Soup with Shrimp

7 Drinks

122   Masala Crab Salad
      with Mango

124   Mini Shepherd's Pies

126   Kir Royale Floats

127   Butterscotch Panna Cotta

128   Coconut–Star Anise
      Rice Pudding

130   Manhattans with
      Spiced Cherries

131   Fresh Greyhounds

132   Rosemary Martinis

134   Lava Lounge Punch

136   Strawberry-Ginger
      Champagne Cocktails

137   Bloody Marys with
      Fresh Horseradish

138   Pomegranate-Mint Fizz

140   Key Lime Gimlet Cocktails

141   Orange Negronis

142   Watermelon-Rosé Sangria

143   Mocha Almond Java

144   **Appendix:
      Game Stor**

146   **Index**

Acknowledgments

Hearty thanks go out to all the friends and family who have made game night at my house such a pleasure over the years, particularly to those who took part in test runs for the book, scrutinizing all of these recipes in real-world scenarios. Tough work, but thankfully someone was willing to do it! Without them, it would have been just my husband and me playing lots and lots of games of cribbage, Scrabble, and Blokus. Not that I don't love playing games with him! In fact I look forward to beating him at cribbage still when we're 100. No better partner for games, or for life, than Bob.

Cathy Sander's help with the recipe testing was a godsend. And a huge thanks to Susan Volland (great friend and manic Bananagrammer) for casting a keen eye over the recipes and offering valuable feedback.

Finally, thanks to all those in the world of games who shared with me their perspectives on the lives and times of the board game industry today. No flood of new technology will be enough to keep us from gathering around the table to play games. Game developers, retailers, and other enthusiasts are a passionate bunch who will make sure of it.

Are you game?

I bet you are.

Board games have been gaining time in the spotlight in this first slice of the 21st century—independent game stores opening, board games popping up in pop culture and mainstream media, department and home stores showcasing classic games. In fact, just as I was putting finishing touches on this book, *Fortune* magazine reported online that board game sales had seen a nearly 25 percent jump the previous year, with more growth expected for the coming year. That makes it likely that you, dear reader, have found yourself around a table playing a game with some friends not too long ago.

And because most game playing—if you're doing it right—is a leisurely activity that lasts a few hours, food will come into play at some point. All that dice tossing, brain teasing, and creative energy spent bluffing your friends . . . a person needs sustenance to get through it.

This is where the logistical challenge comes in: when game play meets good food. Sticky, greasy fingers can mess up game pieces (not to mention mark cards!). Table space needed for the board, cards, chips, and other game accoutrements makes large dinner plates unreasonable. And the manual element of play makes knife-and-fork eating inconvenient and distracting. Game-friendly treats come to the rescue.

Casual game playing is one thing. A rainy Saturday afternoon spent playing Scrabble, with a plate of chocolate chip cookies and a pot of tea nearby? No problem there. Or an after-dinner game of Pictionary, when all is cleared but the wine glasses, and guests play for an hour before meandering home—that's a scenario that doesn't necessarily need the help this book offers, though recipes here will certainly make those afternoon snacks or after-dinner sweets more interesting.

This book focuses instead on occasions when game playing is the core of the evening. You'll find eighty recipes that make eating well a neat and tidy prospect, keeping hands clean and unencumbered. Guests can easily flip dominoes, handle their Monopoly riches, shuffle cards, and sculpt a masterpiece out of brilliantly purple Cranium clay while eating just as well as they would at any dinner party.

Many factors are bringing tabletop games back into our lives, but I see two key motivators behind the trend. One is a general backlash against the realities of contemporary life. The more our daily existence requires us to be plugged in and electrified—from the first check of email in the morning to the last tweet of the day—the more appealing it is that our downtime come "no batteries required" (excepting perhaps the AA battery needed to light the patient's nose in Operation). And with the economy taking so many dramatic twists and turns in recent years, sticking close to the hearth for homespun entertaining becomes an increasingly attractive prospect.

Having grown up in an avid game-playing family, I took particular note a few years ago when I began reading in national press about the new wave of interest in board games. A December 2003 *New York Times* holiday shopping piece pointed out that "Board games are much in evidence this holiday season . . . pleasingly corrective, it seems, to high-tech gadgets and video games." A month later, I read in the *Wall Street Journal* of the "Canasta Comeback," the article saying that "from San Francisco to Tampa, the hip crowd is embracing the pastimes of a quieter era—starting dominoes clubs, pulling out the backgammon board after dinner parties and installing backyard shuffleboard courts." And one national magazine even became part of the trend with the release of the New Yorker Cartoon Caption Game in 2006.

One of my favorite bedtime reads, *Vanity Fair* magazine, has also touched on the rediscovery of games, beyond even the whole celebrities-playing-poker phenomenon earlier in the 2000s. In one 2007 item, the magazine touted "the game everyone's playing" as dominoes, citing Mexican train as the favored version. (At my house we prefer chicken foot; the same set of double-12 dominoes with a different method of play.)

In a 2008 issue, *Vanity Fair* featured a one-page celebration of the "Return of the Dinner Party," saying that "entertaining at home is back in fashion. . . . Good food, generous cocktails, a little night music and after-dinner games all make for a deliciously delightful evening." On the subject of game night, the magazine explains the MO as such: "Game night at someone's home starts with drinks and dinner . . . and then straight to the dominoes."

This is where I respectfully disagree. When it's game night at my house, the games, dinner, and drinks intermingle completely.

The evening begins with the catch-up time, visiting with friends as they arrive and unwind while the first round of drinks gets poured. A self-serve spread of game-friendly fare is already in place on the kitchen counter. Before long, we choose one of the games from the closet (games are so big at my house that we converted the hall linen closet into the game closet), opening the box of dominoes, spreading out the Balderdash board, or gearing up for a hot game of 2500 (an addictive card game).

If it's a small crowd, six or eight, we'll all play together around the dining room table. When in the mood for a little variety, we may play a few different games in one evening. By setting a one-hour limit for each game, I guarantee no one winner gets to have all the fun, and those games that tend to linger longer—Trivial Pursuit, chicken foot dominoes—don't get a chance to feel tedious. It can become a sort of mini tournament: players earn points based on their rank when time runs out, with prizes at the end of the night for the guests with the most points.

For larger game-night parties, we set out a dozen games on the coffee table, and set up extra tables both in the living/dining area and in the basement (our "Lava Lounge" party room). Then guests pick and choose what they'd like to play, and bounce around from one game to the next. There may be a pair playing cribbage at a card table, a game of dominoes on the dining room table, Apples to Apples and Blokus on tables downstairs, while a couple of folks play a game of pool. And everyone has a small plate laden with delectable food that won't in any way interfere with the game at hand.

It's all about unplugging, reconnecting, finding pleasure and diversion in our own homes, with our friends and family. When the economy pinches, entertaining at home beats an expensive (and frankly often less fun) dinner out. When our daily lives are so plugged in, retreating from the din to relax matters even more.

GETTING GAME

Games of all sorts have woven in and out of my life for many years. When I was a kid, my family played a lot of cribbage and gin rummy, not only at home but on the road as well. Our vacations were often camping and backpacking trips, with a pack of mini cards and a little folding cribbage board easily slipped into the side pocket of a bag. One particularly rainy backpacking trip kept us holed up in one camp spot for a couple of days. We'd forgotten the playing cards, but I cut up some paper from a small notepad I'd taken along, crafting handmade cards to help make the drippy hours pass.

Another favorite game in our family was Tripoley, a betting game with cards and chips that combines poker with Michigan rummy. I inherited the plastic Tripoley mat we unfurled on the dining room table so many times over the decades. It's a game that I had let slip from my repertoire as newer games took center stage. Not long ago, though, we had my sister and her husband over and played Tripoley for the first time in ages (the first time ever for my brother-in-law). My sister glanced at the newer modular Tripoley board someone gave us recently, then looked up at me, quiet for a moment. "Don't you have the old plastic thing?" she asked, hopefully. Away went the new-fangled board and out came the old, well-loved piece of plastic that my family's hands had touched countless times.

Perhaps it's little surprise that, as a writer, I'm now particularly fond of word-related games. We play a lot of Scrabble and Boggle around here, and Quiddler is a recent addition that's lots of fun. I love doing crossword puzzles and Jumbles. In fact, in college—back when I still thought I was going to be an engineer—I was part of a Boggle team in the registrar's office where I worked.

One event that helped fuel my enthusiasm for sharing my love of games was the opening of Blue Highway Games in Seattle in 2007. Their shelves hold nothing electronic, a fact made a bit more meaningful given that the two founders are former computer game developers. They were confident about the future of low-tech tabletop games despite the unending stream of new electronic games being released. Their confidence in turn made me believe that there must be plenty of folks like me who relish the fun of playing games as much as the joys of great food. (I came to find there are a number of stores like Blue Highway in the country, enough to warrant a brief selection of them in the Appendix, page 144.)

Proving that there's something to this food-meets-games crossover is the growing category of food-themed games coming on the market. So much so that the national cookware chain Sur La Table added games to their inventory in 2007, with Foodie Fight a consistent top-seller. You'll see a brief profile of that game on page 23, and profiles of a few other "gastro games" throughout the book.

In the following pages, you'll get the score on planning the food side of a delicious game night, but it's good to give some thought to the game selection as well, choosing the right game for the right group. As enthusiastic as some guests may be about playing Scrabble or Bananagrams, it can be as much a turn-off for those who can't fathom spelling as "fun." Word and trivia games can have pro/con camps, though the latter often allow for team play, which at least doesn't put individuals on the spot. Some good middle-of-the-road options for a mixed crowd, or folks you may not know quite as well, include dominoes, Yahtzee, Apples to Apples, Say Anything, and many card games.

You and your guests might well be surprised at the creativity that lurks in the unexpected crannies of our game-playing selves. Imaginative games like Wise and Otherwise, Balderdash, and New Yorker Cartoon Caption Game can bring out some distinct right-brain revelations in the most left-brained of your friends. Turns out my husband, the software-architect-computer type, is a crack whiz at clever cartoon captions—who knew?

One serious recommendation: Don't sit down to a new still-cellophane-wrapped game on a game night, cracking it open for the first time with guests waiting expectantly for the fun to begin. Unless you (a) know for certain that it's a 5-minutes-or-less-to-learn game or (b) it's one that you've played a few times at someone else's house, opening it just before your first round of play is a bad idea. Nothing takes the air out of good game-night momentum more than stumbling through rules, figuring out the board, and assembling the game pieces. When you buy a new game, open it up, read through the rules, and familiarize yourself with all the ins and outs before having your friends over to join in the fun. Play it a couple of times to get the hang of it, so you can more easily explain the game to others, even if it's a mock game for which you and a friend pretend to be the four needed for play.

I think it's fun to mix things up a bit with the guest list for a game night. Consider various circles of people in your life: school friends, current and former colleagues, family, neighbors. As with any good dinner party, it's nice to have some crossover. I've noticed many occasions when friends and family who have spent plenty of time chatting at our larger parties over the years connect at a whole new level when just six of us are sitting around the dinner table playing games.

ABOUT THE RECIPES

There are plenty of foods that you can eat while playing games: anything from pretzels and sandwiches to sushi and burgers. Decent selections, but there is so much more you can offer your friends beyond the run-of-the-mill and grab-and-go menu of most game-night fare. In the following pages you'll find some familiar favorites done up with a twist, such as Oven Baked Potato Chips with Onion Dip (page 22), Lamb Burgers with Feta (page 83), and Homemade Pretzel Sticks with Three Mustards (page 27). Popular treats such as pizza, banana bread, BLTs, and even Caesar salad are given the game-night treatment as well. And plenty of fresh ideas await, including Wasabi Pea–Crusted Tuna (page 41), Petits Croque Monsieurs (page 76), and Brown Butter Pound Cake with Caramel Dip (page 34).

You'll see that the recipe yields are not listed in the traditional "servings" format. Instead I tell you how many individual portions are made: 12 skewers, 24 tartlets, 8 mini soups, 24 stuffed mushrooms. It's because the number of individuals you can serve from each recipe is intended to be flexible. If you have a large spread with a variety of dishes, one or two mushrooms per person may suffice. But for a smaller group, you may count four or five per serving, with only a couple other dishes on the menu.

I give you a few tools within the recipes to steer you to the best choices for the game night at hand. With "up" (▲) and "down" (▼) you can quickly see to what degree the recipe can easily be adjusted to accommodate varying sizes of gatherings. And "advance" (☺) gives you a heads-up about how much the recipe can be prepped ahead, to help particularly with those larger parties for which advance preparation is so critical.

SUPREME SHORTCUTS

Schedule crazy, time tight, think you can't swing planning a game night? Balderdash. There are some amazing game-friendly shortcuts available to make whipping together a delicious gathering surprisingly easy. When it's Friday morning of a particularly draining week, call your pals and know that you can put on a great spread with what little energy the week has left you.

- Buy a loaf of cocktail bread, a package of cream cheese, and ½ pound of crabmeat. Mush together the cream cheese and crab, season with salt, Tabasco, and fresh chopped herbs if you have them. Spread (not too thick) on the bread, broil for a couple of minutes, and serve.
- Buy a tub of pesto, a tub of sour cream, a bag of baby carrots, a bunch of radishes, and a couple cucumbers. Stir a few spoonfuls of the pesto into the sour cream and put it in small dishes. Trim and rinse the radishes and cut the cucumbers into slices or sticks. Arrange them on a plate with the carrots, setting the dips alongside for each to take.
- Buy a couple packages of Chinese-style barbecued pork (sliced, if possible), along with that fiery mustard commonly served with the pork, and a bunch of green onions. Thinly slice 3 or 4 of the green onions when you get home. Slice a baguette, top each slice with a piece of pork, a smidge of the mustard, and a nice sprinkling of the green onion.
- Add bowls of olives, toasted nuts, and chips that you picked up at the store, and you're not doing too badly for a last-minute, but still tasty, game night. And this is just one example.

Of recipes in this book, here are some you'll want to turn to when time is of the essence.

SAGE POPCORN (page 111)

ARTICHOKE-STUFFED MUSHROOMS (page 56)

CELERY, RADISH, AND PARSLEY SALAD WITH LEMON DRESSING (page 116)

GREEN PEA AND MINT SPREAD WITH CRISPY PANCETTA (page 30)

HERB-MARINATED SHRIMP (page 43)

RADISHES WITH A TRIO OF DIPS (page 24) (the Green Goddess and Blue Cheese dips are quickest to make)

CHILLED AVOCADO SOUP WITH ROASTED POBLANO CREAM (page 112) (skip the roasted poblanos and top with cumin-spiced sour cream)

BEEF YAKITORI (page 50) (cut the marinating time to 30 minutes)

SWORDFISH AND FENNEL SKEWERS (page 45) (cut the marinating time to 30 minutes)

CHOCOLATE TARTLETS WITH BRANDY CREAM (page 105) (skip the brandy cream and top with whipped cream)

BUTTERSCOTCH PANNA COTTA (page 127) (as long as you have the few hours chill time for them to set)

POMEGRANATE MINT FIZZ (page 138)

ORANGE NEGRONIS (page 141)

MOCHA ALMOND JAVA (page 143)

THE ESSENTIALS

I created this book's recipes with game-night ease in mind. But a big part of what's going to make game night as smooth, easy, and mess-free as possible is the serving pieces. You'll find many of these great game-friendly serving items in cookware stores, department stores, and national chains, such as Cost Plus World Market. To stock up for larger game-night gatherings, I recommend checking out restaurant supply stores in your area. You can often find volume packs of glasses, dishes, bamboo skewers, and other serving pieces at very reasonable prices, though selection may be limited to basic styles and colors.

Having these items on hand makes it easy for you to adapt many of your favorite recipes to game night. Smooth soups can be served in espresso cups. You can scoop mini ice cream sundaes into small ramekins. Or bake your favorite bread pudding recipe or macaroni and cheese in individual small dishes instead of one big one.

SMALL RAMEKINS AND/OR BOWLS. Those of ¼- to ½-cup capacity are ideal, and suit a wide range of uses, including baked dishes such as Mini Shepherd's Pies (page 124), or as serving dishes for soups, dips, salads, and desserts.

OTHER RANDOM SMALL DISHES. Some stores offer a treasure trove of small dishes for game-night needs. Be on the lookout for mini gratin dishes, mini boat-shaped dishes, and mini crème brûlée dishes—among others. They'll come in handy for a variety of uses, such as nuts, salads, and popcorn.

PORCELAIN SOUP SPOONS. I fell in love with these as a game-night option, the flat-bottomed spoons often used for wonton and other Asian soups. I serve a number of different salads in these spoons, which guests can enjoy in one tidy mouthful. And you can alter the presentation of other recipes to serve in bite-sized portions for a larger crowd. Consider nixing the bread from the Chicken Salad Sandwiches with Orange and Walnuts (page 77) and serve the salad on spoons instead. Or slice the Grilled Garlicky Mushrooms (page 40) and serve a few slices in a spoon instead of serving them whole on a small pick.

SHOT GLASSES, CORDIAL GLASSES, AND ESPRESSO CUPS. These offer an array of serving options for the more liquid of the recipes. Dips, soups, and, of course, beverages can be served in these versatile dishes, which can range in capacity from ¼ cup to ½ cup. The Butterscotch Panna Cotta (page 127) can be served in these glasses as well, and heatproof espresso cups even can double as smaller-sized baking dishes for a recipe such as the Coconut–Star Anise Rice Pudding (page 128).

SKEWERS AND PICKS. Skewers and picks come in handy for many of the preparations in this book. For serving, you won't want a skewer any longer than 6 inches, so it's not unwieldy on the plate. There are many types of smaller picks available that are great options for presentation, from slim little bamboo picks with a knot at the top to the classic colorful frilly toothpick. For game night, they pierce single Spicy Meatballs with Yogurt-Cucumber Dip (page 46), hold Pickled Grape and Blue Cheese Skewers (page 39), and secure the Itty Bitty BLTs (page 78).

STEMLESS WINE AND MARTINI GLASSES. Long-stemmed glasses on a game table are just asking for trouble: one flourish from the dealer or misdirected pass of the box of questions, and you can have a serious spill on your hands. An increasing variety of wine and cocktail glasses can now be found without stems, which will help avoid spillage. I sometimes even serve wine in sleek little tumblers for a safe, unfussy option.

CRINKLY PAPER CUPS. Traditionally used for lining cupcake pans, paper cups now come in a range of sizes and styles. They work beautifully as convenient serving pieces for snacky items such as Sage Popcorn (page 111) and Cumin Spiced Nuts (page 110). Both have coatings that could interfere with the clean-finger principle, but your guests can just lift the paper cups to their mouths and shake out a few bits at a time to nibble.

SMALL SPOONS AND FORKS. For the few recipes that require a utensil for eating—including Mini Shepherd's Pies (page 124), Butterscotch Panna Cotta (page 127), Coconut–Star Anise Rice Pudding (page 128)—opt for smaller hors d'oeuvres/cocktail forks and small spoons, if possible. Or at least use the smallest flatware you have.

BASIC TECHNIQUES

As for cooking techniques, here are a few essentials that pop up in a number of recipes.

PURÉEING. I rely on the food processor for many recipes in this collection. It's a tool I use so often that it lives on my counter, at the ready any time I need to purée a soup or make a quick batch of hummus. In fact, I have a hard time imagining my cooking routines without a food processor. For some recipes, chopping ingredients by hand may be an alternative, for others perhaps making a paste in a mortar and pestle will work. But for as much use as I get out of this small appliance, I think my trusty processor is one of the best investments I've made in my kitchen. There are times, however, when the best tool for the job is the blender. The Green Gazpacho recipe on page 114 is one of those cases, when the goal is to attain a very smooth, fine texture from the vegetables. Something about the engineering of the blender blades and container assure a smoother result than most food processors will produce.

ROASTING GARLIC. Remove the outer papery skin from a whole head of garlic and cut off the top ¼ inch or so to expose the tops of the cloves. Set the garlic in a piece of aluminum foil and drizzle about 2 teaspoons of olive oil over. If you have fresh thyme on hand, add a few sprigs of that as well. Wrap the foil around the garlic to fully enclose it. Bake in a 375°F oven until the garlic is tender when squeezed, 30 to 40 minutes. Set aside to cool, then squeeze each garlic clove from the bottom to release it from the skin. For a purée simply mash the garlic with a fork. Extra garlic can be wrapped and refrigerated for 4 to 5 days. It will be delicious in pasta, mashed with butter for toasted garlic bread, or added to a vinaigrette for delicate garlicky flavor. In fact, you might want to roast two heads of garlic at once, to have plenty to enjoy for a few other meals.

MAKING SIMPLE SUGAR SYRUP. This simple syrup can be used to add a touch of sweetness to cocktails, iced tea, and other cold beverages. Combine 1 cup water and ¾ cup sugar in a small saucepan and bring to a boil over medium-high heat, stirring to help the sugar dissolve. Boil for 1 minute, then set the pan aside to cool completely before using. Makes about ¾ cup. Refrigerate any extra in an airtight container for up to 2 weeks.

TOASTING NUTS. When a recipe calls for "chopped toasted" nuts, toast the nuts whole and then chop them. It's hard to toast chopped nuts evenly; the smallest pieces risk burning before the larger pieces are toasty. Scatter the nuts in a baking pan (I typically use a metal cake pan) and toast in a 350°F oven until lightly browned and aromatic, stirring the nuts or shaking the pan a few times to encourage even toasting. Smaller nuts, such as slivered almonds and pine nuts, may take just 5 to 7 minutes. Larger, dense nuts may take 10 to 12 minutes. Toasting also helps separate the thin, papery skin from hazelnuts. When you take toasted hazelnuts from the oven, put them in a clean dish towel right away, wrap the towel up around them, and let sit for about 15 minutes. Rub the towel against the nuts to remove the skins. Note that the skins can stain, so consider using a dark-colored towel.

SERVING TIPS

Encourage your friends to graze on game night. Set out plates that are just 7 to 8 inches in size and suggest guests select a few items at a time. No need to overload the plate and have things dripping off the side with the spread close at hand for replenishing. The goal is to keep the food's footprint on the game table to a minimum.

For a smaller crowd and a handful of recipes, go ahead and put everything out at once just as guests are showing up. But for a bigger group and larger menu, consider setting foods out in waves, starting with lighter/cold/snacky items at the beginning, then moving on to more filling salads/seafoods/meats an hour later, with sweets to finish. There's no rush at all, no need to get the eating out of the way. A languorous, easygoing pace encourages your friends to nibble and relax—it's the whole point of an integrated food-and-games night!

Your game-night gatherings will not be like a typical dinner party at which you serve one course at a time, soups kept warm on the stove until ladling into bowls, meats cooked just before serving. Instead these soirees will be more like cocktail parties or buffet suppers, with foods set out for guests to serve themselves a few times over the course of a couple of hours. This brings into play the need for attention to food safety issues, particularly with regard to safe temperatures. Cold foods should be kept cold (below 40°F) and hot foods kept hot (above 140°F). The amount of time food spends in that 40° to 140°F zone should be limited to 2 hours.

As you'll see in many recipes, unless the dish is to be served right away, I recommend refrigerating until you are ready to serve. This may mean the need to reheat in the oven before serving, or letting it come to room temperature to reach the proper consistency. Just try not to overdo the amount of time food is sitting out. Of course, you can be more lenient with less perishable foods, such as the Olive and Cheese Crackers (page 97) or Pickled Grape and Blue Cheese Skewers (page 39). But it always pays to play it safe. If the Shrimp Cakes in Shiso Leaves (page 66) or Pimento Cheese Tower Sandwiches (page 80) have been sitting out for an hour or more, you may want to pop them in the fridge or oven until your guests are ready for more.

Two recipes in this book feature raw seafood, the Tuna Tartare on Daikon Slices (page 58) and Salmon Poke in Endive Leaves (page 60). For the tuna, choose a high-quality sashimi-grade tuna from a reputable seafood market. The salmon you choose should have been previously frozen. Raw, never-frozen salmon is safe if it will be fully cooked before eating, but in the raw state even top sushi chefs use only previously frozen salmon to serve raw.

Consider investing in a countertop warming tray or griddle. I found this an easy way to keep warm foods warm over the course of an hour or longer, not only so they'll taste their best but to help keep food at safer temperatures. You will likely find this appliance beneficial for other situations as well. Cooking loads of flapjacks for brunch perhaps?

When arranging items on a platter, think about providing easy access for clean fingers. For example, have the skewer ends radiate out from the center of the platter, or arrange the broad unadorned end of a pita wedge toward your guests for easy pickup.

MENU PLANNING

Game night can mean anything from a quiet evening for two to a spirited gathering with a couple dozen friends, and many engaging, dynamic scenarios in between. Recipes in this book tend to have a group in mind, with yields that will mix-and-match well for eight to twelve guests. But the beauty of many of the recipes is the flexibility they offer, so you can easily accommodate a larger or smaller gathering.

For example, the Lentil and Carrot Soup with Cilantro Purée (page 115) serves eight in ½-cup portions, but doubles to sixteen servings if you present it in smaller ¼-cup capacity glasses instead. It's one of many scalability tips you'll find in the recipe chapters. On the flip side, consider the Fennel and Corn Salad (page 118). Served in small bite-sized portions on porcelain spoons, the recipe is an ideal choice for a large group. But if you have six for dinner instead, simply serve larger portions of the salad in ramekins or other small dishes.

A general tip for menu planning is to shoot for variety. If the evening features hearts or bridge, the four of you can enjoy a savory pastry or snack, a crisp vegetable item, one substantial meat or seafood recipe, and a bite of something sweet to finish. For a crowd, you'll want a few snacky items, perhaps two lighter vegetable or seafood items, two more filling meat dishes, and a couple of desserts to cap things off. You'll find hints in the recipes about which items are best for which scenarios. Make-ahead and easily doubled recipes will go far to make your workload easier when entertaining larger crowds.

Remember this is grown-up grazing: a delicious cross between cocktail party nibbling and a full dinner party. The individual portions may be small but the overall effect will be one of complete satisfaction for your game-night guests. It adds up to fun times and great food going hand in hand.

GAME NIGHT FOR TWO

YOU MIGHT BE PLAYING

Backgammon	Battleship	Checkers
Chess	Chinese checkers	Cribbage
Go	Mancala	Mastermind
	Stratego	

WHAT YOU MIGHT WANT TO SERVE

For an intimate tête-à-tête game night, you'll likely want to scale down the recipes so you don't have a whopping amount of leftovers. Unless that's part of your scheme—items such as Spicy Meatballs with Yogurt-Cucumber Dip (page 46) and Brown Butter Pound Cake with Caramel Dip (page 34) are good candidates because leftovers will keep well for a few days.

POMEGRANATE-MINT FIZZ (page 138):
halve the recipe or chill extra for refills

WASABI PEA–CRUSTED TUNA (page 41):
a good serving for two or halve the recipe

ITTY BITTY BLTs (page 78):
halve the recipe to make six mini sandwiches

RADISHES WITH A TRIO OF DIPS (page 24):
choose just one dip and use one bunch of radishes

RASPBERRY AND CREAM CHEESE TURNOVERS (page 108):
freeze extra to have on hand for a quick dessert another time

GAME NIGHT FOR TWO TO FOUR

YOU MIGHT BE PLAYING

Blokus	Boggle	Bridge
Canasta	The Game of Life	Hearts
Mah-jongg	Parcheesi	Pinochle
Scrabble	Settlers of Catan	Ticket to Ride

WHAT YOU MIGHT WANT TO SERVE

As noted for the two-person meal, many recipes in this book will have a larger yield than needed for two to four players. Of course, you can choose to increase the per-person serving size of each recipe—such as four or five of the Chicken Salad Sandwiches with Orange and Walnuts (page 77) or Beef Yakitori skewers (page 50) per person—to accommodate the smaller group.

ROSEMARY MARTINIS (page 132):
halve the recipe or chill extra for refills

SALMON POKE IN ENDIVE LEAVES (page 60):
halve the recipe for twelve portions

OVEN-BAKED POTATO CHIPS WITH ONION DIP (page 22)

LAMB AND OLIVE KEBABS (page 48)

NUTELLA AND BANANA GALETTES (page 106):
bake pastry rounds from half the dough; freeze the rest
for a future Nutella-craving emergency

GAME NIGHT FOR UP TO EIGHT

Clue	Dominoes	Foodie Fight
Mental Floss	New Yorker Cartoon Caption Game	Monopoly
Operation	Risk	Tripoley
Uno	Wise and Otherwise	Wit's End
	Yahtzee	

WHAT YOU MIGHT WANT TO SERVE

Most of the recipes in this book will work well for this number of guests, though those that make a large number of individual portions, such as the Herbed Biscuits with Smoked Salmon (page 59) and Chocolate Tartlets with Brandy Cream (page 105), should probably be saved for a larger group to avoid leftovers.

ORANGE NEGRONIS (page 141):
consider a double batch to be ready for seconds

PICKLED GRAPE AND BLUE CHEESE SKEWERS (page 39)

ARTICHOKE-STUFFED MUSHROOMS (page 56)

CHILLED AVOCADO SOUP WITH ROASTED POBLANO CREAM (page 112)

ALMOST BITE-SIZED PIZZAS (page 95)

LAMB BURGERS WITH FETA (page 83)

PERSONAL CHOCOLATE-PORT FONDUES (page 36)

GAME NIGHT FOR A CROWD

Many games can (if not should) be played in teams, which allows good flexibility with regard to number of players, so you can play with as few as two or as many as a dozen. For gatherings with much more than a dozen guests, I recommend you plan on a few games from the previous lists to be played concurrently. Even the best party game played in a large group can get a little clunky.

YOU MIGHT BE PLAYING

| Apples to Apples | Charades | Cranium |
| Pictionary | Poker | Trivial Pursuit |

WHAT YOU MIGHT WANT TO SERVE

Be sure to pick some do-ahead items for a big bash, to reduce your workload the day of the party. Any that can be frozen or refrigerated for a day or two are prime candidates. Also consider dishes that don't require much last-minute prep or assembly just before serving. Invite one or two of your game-playing pals to help with any final cooking and plating!

LAVA LOUNGE PUNCH (page 134):
consider making a double batch

MANHATTANS WITH SPICED CHERRIES (page 130):
consider making a double batch

OLIVE AND CHEESE CRACKERS (page 97)

CUMIN SPICED NUTS (page 110)

CELERY, RADISH, AND PARSLEY SALAD WITH LEMON DRESSING (page 116)

HERBED BISCUITS WITH SMOKED SALMON (page 59)

BEEF EMPANADAS WITH BLACK BEANS AND JALAPEÑO (page 100)

PORK TENDERLOIN WITH RHUBARB CHUTNEY (page 81)

WALNUT SABLÉS WITH MAPLE-WALNUT CREAM (page 84)

PB&J BLONDIE BITES (page 86)

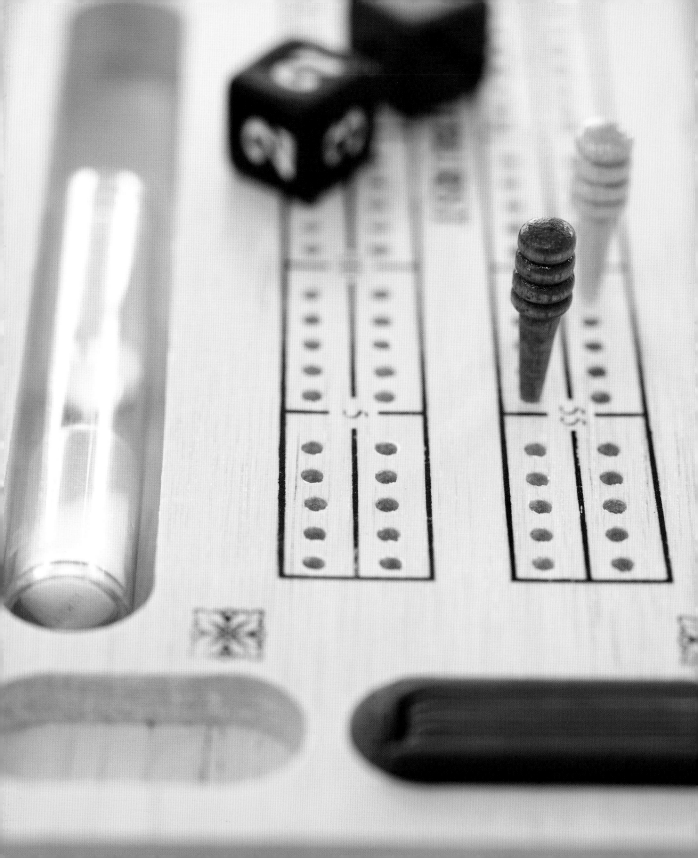

1 DIPS AND SPREADS

Dips and spreads kick off this collection of game-friendly dishes with recipes that offer full flavor in small packages. And they just scratch the surface as examples of how well you can eat by topping a toasted slice of baguette with something savory or by taking a fresh look at fondue and onion dip. Dunking is a supremely satisfying act of eating. My guess is it's because of some primal connection to our ancestors melded with the fact that eating with our fingers flies in the face of table etiquette. I bet you'll have a lot more fun eating the Caesar rendition that follows than you will the next time you dig into one with a knife and fork.

Caesar Dip with Big Croutons and Romaine

When I served this at one of my test-run game nights, friends were dipping pretty much everything in sight into the Caesar dip. Even the occasional finger, though that breaks with the precepts of clean-finger fare. Use a spoon, people!

For this recipe the crouton strips shouldn't get quite as crunchy as a classic crouton, so your guests can easily bite into them without much crumbling. Choose a white or just lightly sour style of rustic bread. The romaine will lose some of its crispness after an hour or so; keep it wrapped in damp paper towels in the fridge until ready to serve.

1 (1½-pound) round loaf
　　artisan bread

1 large head romaine lettuce,
　　trimmed

CAESAR DIP

¼ cup freshly grated Parmesan
　　cheese

1¼ cups top-quality mayonnaise

½ cup freshly squeezed lemon juice

2 to 3 anchovy fillets

3 cloves garlic, minced or pressed

Salt and freshly ground black pepper

Preheat the broiler and set the oven rack about 6 inches below the heating element.

Cut 4 slices from the center of the bread loaf, each ¾ inch thick, saving the rest for another use. Cut the bread slices across into strips about 3 inches long and ¾ inch wide (you should have about 24 strips). Arrange the strips on a baking sheet and broil until lightly browned and crisp, 3 to 4 minutes, turning the pieces halfway through. Set aside to cool.

To make the dip, pulse the Parmesan cheese a few times in a food processor to finely mince it. Add the mayonnaise, lemon juice, anchovy fillets, and garlic and process until smooth. Taste the dressing for seasoning, adding salt (if needed) and pepper to taste. Refrigerate until you are ready to serve.

Use the romaine leaves that measure 5 to 10 inches in length for this recipe, saving the rest for another use. The smaller, most tender leaves can be served whole. Halve larger leaves length-wise, removing the central rib as you do so.

To serve, pour the dip into 8 shot glasses or other small dishes of about ¼-cup capacity and put the croutons in a bowl. Set these on a platter surrounded by the romaine leaves. Your guests should take a dip of their own, helping themselves to the dippers.

MAKES 8 MINI SALADS

▲ Double or triple all the ingredients.

▼ Halve all the ingredients, but a mini processor will work best with those quantities. Or make the full dip recipe and save the extra for another use.

☺ Prepare all the components up to 1 day ahead: store the croutons in an airtight container, store lettuce wrapped in damp paper towels in the refrigerator, and store the dip in an airtight container in the refrigerator.

Edamame Purée in Cherry Tomatoes

Cherry tomatoes are one of nature's best edible containers. You can stuff them with any number of delicious fillings, including pretty much anything in the "salad" family—chicken salad, tuna salad, egg salad—or fresh goat cheese blended with lots of fresh herbs. If you want to get creative, you can make two different fillings and use the stuffed tomatoes as edible checker pieces.

It's a time-saver to use shelled edamame for this recipe. But the flavor will be a bit better if you buy the beans with shells and shell them after cooking (follow instructions on the bag). A 12-ounce bag of in-shell beans should give you just the 1 cup needed here.

1 cup shelled edamame beans

2 tablespoons chopped fresh cilantro

2 tablespoons freshly squeezed lemon juice

1 tablespoon Asian sesame oil

1 teaspoon soy sauce

1 clove garlic, minced or pressed

1 to 3 teaspoons water, as needed

About 24 cherry tomatoes

1 tablespoon toasted sesame seeds

Bring a small pan of salted water to a boil. Add the edamame and boil for 1 minute. Drain and let cool.

Combine the edamame, cilantro, lemon juice, sesame oil, soy sauce, and garlic in a food processor and purée until smooth, scraping down the sides as needed. The purée should be thick enough to hold its shape but not too stiff; add a teaspoon or two of water and pulse a few times if needed. Refrigerate until you are ready to stuff the tomatoes.

Cut about ¼ inch from the top of each cherry tomato and use a small spoon to scoop out the flesh and seeds from the interior; discard or add to a batch of tomato sauce. Set the tomatoes upside down on a double layer of paper towels and let drain for about 30 minutes.

To serve, spoon the edamame purée into the cherry tomatoes, sprinkle with the sesame seeds, and arrange them on a platter.

MAKES ABOUT 24 STUFFED TOMATOES

▲ Double all the ingredients.
▼ Halve all the ingredients.
☉ Stuff the tomatoes up to 4 hours ahead; cover and refrigerate. Top with sesame seeds just before serving.

Crostini with Wild Mushroom Tapenade

This recipe replaces the traditional olives in a tapenade with mushrooms—preferably wild—for a slightly earthier variation. When wild mushrooms aren't in season, you can use regular button mushrooms. If so, I recommend adding dried wild mushrooms (porcini would be ideal) to the mix for a boost of flavor.

¾ pound wild mushrooms or button mushrooms, trimmed and coarsely chopped

½ ounce dried wild mushrooms (optional)

4 tablespoons olive oil

¼ cup chopped capers

3 tablespoons finely chopped onion

2 teaspoons minced or pressed garlic

¼ cup finely chopped fresh flat-leaf parsley

2 tablespoons freshly squeezed lemon juice

Salt and freshly ground black pepper

24 baguette slices, lightly toasted

Fried capers, for garnish (optional; see box)

Pulse the fresh mushrooms in a food processor until finely chopped (but not puréed), scraping down the sides once or twice. Soak dried mushrooms in about 1 cup warm water for 30 minutes. Lift out the softened mushrooms and squeeze gently over the bowl; finely chop the mushrooms, reserving the soaking liquid.

Heat 2 tablespoons of the olive oil in a medium skillet over medium heat. Add the fresh mushrooms and cook, stirring occasionally, until they are tender and any liquid they give off has evaporated, about 5 minutes. Pour the mushroom soaking liquid into the skillet, leaving any grit behind in the bowl. Continue cooking until the liquid has evaporated, 7 to 10 minutes. Add the reconstituted mushrooms, capers, onion, and garlic and cook, stirring, until aromatic, 1 to 2 minutes. Remove the skillet from the heat and stir in the parsley and lemon juice. Add salt and pepper to taste. Let cool.

To serve, lightly brush the toasts with the remaining 2 tablespoons of the olive oil. Spread the mushroom mixture onto the toasts and arrange on a platter for serving, topping the toasts with fried capers.

MAKES 24 CROSTINI

▲ Double all the ingredients.
▼ Halve all the ingredients.
☺ Make the mushroom mixture up to 1 day ahead and refrigerate. Assemble the crostini not more than 1 hour before serving.

FRIED CAPERS

Fried capers make a tasty garnish for these crostini, as they will for any dish made with capers, such as veal or chicken piccata. Simply heat a couple tablespoons of olive oil in a small skillet over medium-high heat. Pat a few tablespoons of capers dry with a paper towel and add the capers to the skillet. Stir or toss gently as they cook. After a minute or two, when they are puffed and crispy, transfer them to paper towels to drain.

Oven-Baked Potato Chips with Onion Dip

This is the ultimate American party and game food, even to those for whom "game" brings to mind a baseball scoreboard more than it does a Clue board.

Choose potatoes that have a relatively cylindrical shape consistent from end to end, so that your slices will be pretty even. The blue cheese dip on page 24 is another delicious option for these chips. If you're pressed for time, you can buy some really good potato chips instead of baking your own at home.

ONION DIP

1 tablespoon olive oil

1 medium onion, finely chopped

1½ teaspoons minced fresh thyme, or ½ teaspoon dried

½ cup beef broth, preferably reduced-sodium

2 cloves garlic, minced or pressed

¾ cup top-quality mayonnaise

½ cup sour cream

½ teaspoon Tabasco, or more to taste

Salt

POTATO CHIPS

2 russet potatoes (about 1½ pounds)

2 tablespoons olive oil

Salt

To make the onion dip, heat the olive oil in a medium skillet over medium heat. Add the onion and thyme and cook, stirring often, until the onions are very tender and nicely browned, 10 to 12 minutes. The onions shouldn't brown too fast; reduce the heat to medium-low if needed. Add the broth and garlic and cook until the liquid is completely evaporated, about 5 minutes. Set aside to cool. When cool, stir in the mayonnaise, sour cream, Tabasco, and salt to taste. Transfer the dip to a bowl, cover, and refrigerate until you are ready to serve.

Preheat the oven to 350°F. Line 2 baking sheets with a silicone baking mat or parchment paper. Set 2 oven racks at the centermost levels.

To prepare the potato chips, half-fill a large bowl with cold water. Peel 1 of the potatoes and cut it crosswise into ⅛-inch-thick slices, preferably using a mandoline slicer. Add the slices to the water and repeat with the second potato. Use your hands to swish the potato slices around in the water to remove the excess starch.

Dry the potato slices well on a clean kitchen towel. Rinse and dry the bowl and return the potato slices to it. Drizzle the olive oil over and toss to evenly coat the slices with the oil. Arrange the potato slices in a single layer on the baking sheets and sprinkle lightly with salt. Bake until the slices are lightly browned and crisp, 30 to 40 minutes, turning the slices over and switching the baking sheets about halfway through for even cooking. Keep an eye on the progress near the end; some slices may be done sooner. Transfer them to a wire rack to cool.

To serve, spoon the dip into individual dishes and set them on a platter or tray. Set the chips in a bowl alongside for your guests to serve themselves.

MAKES 8 TO 10 DIPS WITH CHIPS

▲ Double all the ingredients, baking the potatoes in two batches.

▼ Halve all the ingredients.

☺ It is best to make dip at least 4 hours ahead, but it can be made up to 1 day ahead and kept covered and refrigerated. The chips are best made not more than 2 hours before serving.

GASTRO GAMES: FOODIE FIGHT
(Chronicle Books, 2007)

Q: What implement does Jack Lemmon use to strain spaghetti in the film *The Apartment*?
A: A tennis racket.

I have no idea if that question is in the box of trivia cards that comes with Foodie Fight; I haven't been through them all yet. But back in 2005 I started jotting down ideas for a culinary trivia game, though my enthusiasm for the project lasted only as long as it took to come up with some categories and a dozen questions (including the above). So I was pleased, but not at all surprised, when Foodie Fight was released, the "trivia game for serious food lovers." It does an admirable job of covering culinary topics that range from the truly trivial to practical pointers, in a game format that's easy to get the hang of. All in all, a fun choice for the most gastro of your friends.

Radishes with a Trio of Dips

You can serve just one or two of these dips to your guests, but it's fun to go overboard and offer a variety of options. No need to serve some of each dip to every guest. When I have a dozen friends over, I'll put out four dishes of each and let them choose which they would like. If you are making just one or two dips, plan to double the dip recipes. Any extra green goddess or blue cheese dip makes delicious salad dressing. Romesco is wonderful spooned over roasted potatoes.

GREEN GODDESS DIP

½ cup top-quality mayonnaise

2 anchovy fillets, finely chopped

2 tablespoons finely chopped fresh flat-leaf parsley

1 tablespoon minced fresh chives

1 tablespoon tarragon vinegar or white wine vinegar

1½ teaspoons minced fresh tarragon

BLUE CHEESE DIP

½ cup crumbed blue cheese

¼ cup sour cream

3 tablespoons finely chopped green onion, white and pale green parts

2 tablespoons whole milk, plus more if needed

Salt

To make the green goddess dip, combine the mayonnaise, anchovies, parsley, chives, vinegar, and tarragon in a food processor and process until smooth. Cover and refrigerate until you are ready to serve.

To make the blue cheese dip, stir together the blue cheese, sour cream, and green onion until well blended, pressing on the blue cheese chunks with the back of the spoon to break them up. Stir in the milk, 1 tablespoon at a time, enough to make a dippable, not-too-chunky consistency. Season to taste with salt. Cover and refrigerate until you are ready to serve.

To make the romesco dip, roast the red pepper under the broiler until the skin blackens, turning occasionally to roast evenly, 12 to 15 minutes. Put the pepper in a plastic bag, tie it closed, and set aside to cool. When cool enough to handle, peel away and discard the skin. Remove the core and seeds and chop the pepper. Combine the roasted pepper, tomato, almonds, olive oil, garlic, and vinegar in a food processor and process until smooth. If the mixture is quite thick, add a tablespoon or two of water. Season to taste with salt. Cover and refrigerate until you are ready to serve.

To prepare the radishes, trim the greens to about 1 inch in length. Rinse the radishes well and dry on paper towels. If any of the radishes are quite large, carefully halve them so that the green tops are halved as well.

ROMESCO DIP

1 small red bell pepper

$1/2$ cup chopped tomato

$1/3$ cup toasted slivered almonds
(see page 9)

$1/4$ cup olive oil

2 cloves garlic, crushed

1 tablespoon red wine vinegar

Salt

3 bunches radishes, with
their greens

When you are ready to serve, spoon the sauces into small individual bowls. Arrange the radishes in a bowl and set it on a platter or tray, with the dip bowls arranged around the radish bowl.

MAKES 12 DIPS WITH RADISHES

▲ Double or triple all the ingredients.

▼ Make just 1 or 2 of the dips and use 1 or 2 bunches of radishes.

☻ Make the sauces up to 1 day ahead, cover, and refrigerate. Prepare the radishes up to 4 hours ahead, wrap in damp paper towels, and refrigerate.

Homemade Pretzel Sticks with Three Mustards

There's no comparing standard snack-aisle pretzel sticks with these homemade chewy treats. Certainly feel free to buy a few fancy flavored mustards at the store to use for the dips, but these do-it-yourself combinations will have brighter fresh flavor. Offer perhaps four small bowls of each, letting guests pick the flavor they prefer. But don't be surprised when there is long-distance dipping in a neighbor's dish at the table.

PRETZEL STICKS

2 cups all-purpose flour, plus more if needed

2 teaspoons sugar

1 teaspoon salt

¾ cup warm (about 105°F) water

1 teaspoon (½ package) active dry yeast

1 tablespoon baking soda

1 egg yolk

2 tablespoons water

Coarse salt, for finishing

HERBED MUSTARD

½ cup Dijon mustard

2 tablespoons minced tender fresh herbs (chives, flat-leaf parsley, chervil, tarragon, and/or basil)

ROASTED GARLIC MUSTARD

½ cup Dijon mustard

2 tablespoons puréed roasted garlic (see page 9)

SMOKE AND SPICE MUSTARD

½ cup Dijon mustard

1 tablespoon smoked paprika

½ teaspoon cayenne pepper

To make the pretzel sticks, combine the flour, sugar, and salt in a bowl and stir to mix. Make a well in the center. Pour the warm water into the well and sprinkle the yeast over. Set aside until the yeast is frothy, about 5 minutes.

Stir the dough with a wooden spoon, drawing in the flour from the edges. Continue to stir the dough until it begins to come together in a ball. Transfer it to a lightly floured work surface and knead the dough until it becomes smooth and satiny, about 10 minutes, adding a bit more flour if needed. Put the dough in a bowl (it could be the same bowl in which you mixed the dough), cover the bowl with a clean kitchen towel, and set aside in a warm place until the dough has doubled in bulk, about 1 hour.

While the dough is rising, make the mustards. Stir the ingredients for each in a separate small bowl.

Just before the dough has finished rising, fill a large skillet or sauté pan with 2 to 3 inches of water and set it over medium-high heat; reduce the heat to medium-low if it comes to a boil while you're still working on the dough.

Punch down the dough and cut it into about 30 even portions, each roughly the size of a marshmallow. Roll one portion of dough to a stick 7 to 8 inches long. Set on a lightly floured baking sheet and continue with the remaining dough.

Return the water to a boil if needed, add the baking soda, and reduce the heat to medium. Add 8 to 10 of the pretzel sticks to the water and simmer for 1 minute, then roll the pretzels to their other side and simmer 1 minute longer. Lift the pretzels out with tongs or a large slotted spoon to a tray, then arrange them on a wire rack to drain and cool. (I put a dish towel under the rack to catch drips, and excess salt later.) Repeat with the remaining dough, reheating the water between batches as needed.

Preheat the oven to 375°F. Line 2 baking sheets with silicone baking mats or parchment paper. Set 2 oven racks on the center-most levels.

Beat the egg yolk with the water in a small dish. Brush the pretzels with the yolk mixture and sprinkle with coarse salt. Transfer the pretzel sticks to the baking sheets about 1 inch apart. Bake until golden brown, 25 to 30 minutes, switching the trays about halfway through for even cooking. While the pretzels are baking, transfer the mustards to serving bowls.

Let the pretzel sticks cool a bit on a wire rack and then arrange them on a platter or upright in a large glass, slightly warm or at room temperature. Set the bowls of mustards alongside, with spoons for guests to spoon some onto their own plates.

MAKES ABOUT 30 PRETZELS

▲ Make a double batch of pretzel dough. You may have enough mustard with the original recipe amounts.

▼ Best not to halve.

⊙ The pretzels can be baked up to 4 hours before serving. The dips can be made up to 2 days ahead, covered, and refrigerated.

Crostini with Chicken Liver Mousse and Kumquats

If kumquats are not available, you can use fresh or dried figs cut in thin slices. Try to get your hands on a baguette loaf that's slightly dense in texture. Classic baguettes can have sizeable air holes in them, leaving slices with large gaps in them. You don't want that delicious chicken liver mousse to fall through and disrupt your dominoes!

8 ounces chicken livers, rinsed and dried

6 tablespoons unsalted butter, at room temperature

1/2 cup finely chopped shallot or onion

1 teaspoon minced or pressed garlic

Salt and freshly ground black pepper

3 tablespoons brandy

2 tablespoons chicken broth or freshly squeezed orange juice

4 to 5 kumquats

About 30 baguette slices, lightly toasted

Use a small knife to cut away any membrane from the chicken livers. Heat 2 tablespoons of the butter in a skillet over medium heat. Add the shallot and garlic and cook, stirring, until tender and aromatic, 2 to 3 minutes. Add the chicken livers with a good pinch each of salt and pepper and cook, stirring often, until the livers are evenly browned and cooked through (cut into a few pieces; there should be no pink left in the center), 10 to 12 minutes. Add the brandy to the pan. If it flames up, simply shake the pan gently until the flames subside. Cook for 1 minute, then set aside to cool.

Transfer the livers to a food processor, along with all the shallot and other flavorful bits from the skillet. Add the remaining 4 tablespoons butter and the chicken broth. Process until very smooth, scraping down the sides as needed. Transfer the purée to a bowl and taste for seasoning, adding salt and pepper to taste. Cover and refrigerate.

Take the mousse from the refrigerator about 30 minutes before needed, to allow it to soften a bit. Trim the ends from the kumquats and thinly slice them, removing seeds as you go. Spread each toasted baguette slice with about 1 tablespoon of the chicken liver mousse, top with a slice of kumquat, and arrange on a platter or tray for serving.

MAKES ABOUT 30 CROSTINI

▲ Double all the ingredients.
▼ Halve all the ingredients.
⊘ Make the mousse up to 3 days ahead, cover, and refrigerate; assemble not more than 1 hour before serving, cover, and refrigerate.

Green Pea and Mint Spread with Crispy Pancetta

Those Trivial Pursuit wedges eluding you? You can turn to one of these pita wedges while you're waiting for the perfect category.

Sweet green peas make a wonderful purée base, and the flavor is brightened by fresh mint and accented with crisp pancetta. For a vegetarian version, omit the pancetta and top the spread with thin crispy fried slices of shallot.

2 cups fresh or thawed frozen green peas

3 tablespoons chicken or vegetable broth or water, plus more if needed

2 teaspoons finely chopped fresh mint

Salt and freshly ground black pepper

5 thin slices pancetta

2 thick (6-inch) pitas (preferably without pockets)

Bring a pan of salted water to a boil and prepare a bowl of ice water. Add the peas to the boiling water and simmer over medium heat until tender, 2 to 3 minutes for fresh peas, about 1 minute for frozen peas. Drain, add to the ice water, and let cool. Drain the cooled peas and scatter them on paper towels to dry.

Purée the peas, chicken broth, and mint in a food processor until smooth, scraping down the sides as needed. The texture should be firm enough to hold its shape but not stiff; add another teaspoon or two of broth if needed. Season to taste with salt and pepper. Refrigerate, covered, until you are ready to serve.

Heat a skillet over medium heat. Add the pancetta slices and cook until nicely crisp and lightly browned, about 5 minutes, turning the slices occasionally. Drain on paper towels.

Preheat the broiler and set the top rack about 5 inches below the heating element. Set the pitas directly on the rack and broil until lightly browned, 1 to 2 minutes per side (use tongs to turn the pitas easily). Let cool, then cut each round into 12 wedges.

Top the broad end of each pita wedge with about 1 tablespoon of the pea purée. Break the pancetta into bite-sized pieces and press a piece or two into the purée on each wedge. Arrange the wedges on a platter and serve.

MAKES 24 PITA WEDGES

▲ Double or triple all the ingredients, but make the purée in batches.
▼ Halve all the ingredients.
☺ Make the purée up to 1 day ahead, cover, and refrigerate. Toast the pitas and cook the pancetta up to 4 hours ahead. Assemble shortly before serving.

Individual Cheese Fondues with Apples and Ham

Ham and cheese. Apples and cheese. Bread and cheese. Cheese is a phenomenal partner for so many foods. I devised this twist on classic cheese fondue to allow all those combinations to shine.

¾ cup dry white wine

¼ teaspoon minced or pressed garlic

8 ounces Jarlsberg, Emmental, or other Swiss-type cheese, grated (about 3 cups)

4 ounces fontina cheese, grated (about 1½ cups)

1 ounce Parmesan cheese, grated (about ½ cup)

2 teaspoons cornstarch

1 Fuji or Cameo apple or other dessert apple, cored and cut into ½-inch wedges

2 ounces thinly sliced Black Forest or other top-quality ham (about 5 slices)

24 (1-inch) baguette cubes

Combine the wine and garlic in a saucepan over medium heat and bring to a low boil. While the wine is heating, combine the cheeses and cornstarch in a bowl and toss well to evenly mix. Add the cheese mixture to the wine and cook gently, stirring often, until the cheese is fully melted and smooth in texture, 3 to 5 minutes. The mixture should not boil; reduce the heat to medium-low if needed. Keep warm over very low heat.

Halve each apple wedge crosswise. Cut the ham into strips about 1 inch wide and 4 to 5 inches long. Thread a bread cube onto a slender 3- to 4-inch pick or short skewer. Wrap a strip of ham around an apple piece and add it to the pick. Repeat with the remaining bread, apple, and ham; you should have about 24 skewers in all.

Arrange the skewers on a plate. Pour the fondue into the dishes of 6 butter warmers and set them above the candles. Have guests light the candles once they're seated. Each skewer should be enjoyed in 2 bites, first the ham-wrapped apple, then the bread. Double-dipping is allowed with individual fondues!

MAKES 6 FONDUES

▲ Double if you have 12 butter warmers.

▼ Best not to halve.

☺ Quickly dip the apple pieces in a lemon juice/water bath (about 1 cup water with 2 tablespoons lemon juice) and pat dry to avoid discoloration. Then assemble the apple/ham skewers 1 hour ahead and cover well to avoid drying out. The fondue mixture should be made just before serving.

MINI FONDUE POTS

Because the melted cheese for fondue starts to set up pretty quickly as it cools, it's ideal to use a mini fondue setup for each person. "Butter warmers" are perfect, bi-level apparatuses that perch a small dish above a tea light candle—sold with the idea of keeping melted butter warm while eating lobster or steamed artichokes. National housewares chains and cookware stores offer a few different styles, some at surprisingly inexpensive prices.

These butter warmers will also come in handy for the Personal Chocolate-Port Fondues (page 36) though it's less critical there, since the melted chocolate stays dippable on its own much longer.

GASTRO GAMES: CELEBRITY CHEF! THE GAME
(Idea Farm NYC, 2007)

I'm not sure anything proves the mainstream appeal of the celebrity chef more so than a board game devoted to giving us all a turn at being celebrity chefs. Is it today's version of fantasy projection to a life of riches and fame, as was Monopoly back in the 1930s? Instead of real estate and utilities, players work to accumulate cookbook offers, restaurants, television shows, and endorsements. Some progress is earned by answering trivia questions, but there are also a couple fresh elements. For "Name That Dish" players are given a list of ingredients and must name the dish in which they converge. For "Cook Off" a player challenges another to see who comes up with the most examples of a given topic—perhaps "farmers' market foods" or "traditional Thanksgiving dishes." You can try your hand at some sample questions at www.celebrity chefthegame.com.

Brown Butter Pound Cake with Caramel Dip

This cake is like a big ingot of gold. Already-rich pound cake takes on extra panache with the addition of brown butter, which adds a slightly nutty flavor to the moist cake. Though intended as finger food, the cake should be served with small forked bamboo picks or large toothpicks on hand to prevent the sticky fingers that happen when that last nub of the cake is dipped.

For a thicker caramel sauce to use on ice cream, use less heavy cream, about 1 cup.

POUND CAKE

1 cup unsalted butter, at room temperature

1 cup sugar

4 eggs

1 teaspoon pure vanilla extract

1/2 teaspoon salt

1 1/2 cups all-purpose flour, sifted

CARAMEL DIP

1 cup sugar

1/4 cup water

1 1/2 cups whipping cream

1 teaspoon pure vanilla extract

Preheat the oven to 325°F. Butter a 9 by 5-inch loaf pan and line the length of the pan with a strip of parchment paper cut with a couple of inches of excess at either end. Butter the paper as well. (This paper bit is optional but serves as extra insurance against sticking.)

To make the pound cake, melt 1/2 cup of the butter in a small saucepan over medium heat. Continue cooking until the solids in the butter turn a medium brown and the butter smells nutty, 5 to 6 minutes. The butter might sputter a bit, as excess water evaporates. Different brands of butter may take longer to brown, given different compositions. Set the brown butter aside to cool.

Combine the remaining 1/2 cup of the butter and the sugar in the bowl of a stand mixer fitted with the paddle attachment and beat at medium speed until very light and fluffy. Add the eggs, one at a time, beating until each is well incorporated before adding the next. Scrape down the sides of the bowl as needed.

Add the brown butter (be careful to scrape all the flavorful bits from the pan), vanilla, and salt to the batter and blend at low speed to mix. Remove the bowl from the mixer and add the flour in 3 batches, gently but thoroughly folding in each batch by hand before adding the next.

Spoon the batter into the loaf pan, smoothing the surface. Bake until a toothpick inserted in the center comes out clean, about 1 hour. Let cool for a few minutes in the pan, then turn the cake out onto a wire rack and carefully turn it back upright to cool completely.

To make the caramel dip, combine the sugar and water in a high-sided, heavy saucepan and set over medium heat, stirring occasionally, until the sugar has melted. Continue cooking (without stirring) until the sugar turns a deep mahogany color, 8 to 12 minutes; you may see a few tiny wisps of smoke rising from the surface. Take the pan from the heat and carefully but quickly pour about half of the cream into the pan; it will bubble up quite a lot but subside after a few seconds. Add the rest of the cream and the vanilla. Return the pan to medium heat and cook, stirring, until the caramel dip is smooth and slightly thickened, 1 to 2 minutes. Transfer the dip to a bowl and let cool.

To serve, pour the caramel dip into small bowls or glasses and set them to one side of a large plate or platter. Trim the ends from the pound cake and cut it into 1 inch slices. Cut each slice across into ¾-inch fingers, arrange them on the platter and serve.

MAKES 8 TO 10 DIPS WITH CAKE

▲ Double all the ingredients, baking the pound cake in two pans. Use a large saucepan for the caramel dip.

▼ This is hard to halve, but you can serve fewer portions, saving the extra cake (well wrapped) and the extra dip (refrigerated) for another time.

☺ Make the cake and dip up to 2 days ahead; store the cake well wrapped and the dip in the refrigerator. Let the dip come to room temperature before serving.

Personal Chocolate-Port Fondues

We all know how well port goes with chocolate. So why not *in* it? I asked myself. The results are quite a delight. You can use butter warmers (see page 33) to keep the chocolate warm, though it will stay dippable on its own for a while.

8 ounces semisweet chocolate, chopped

⅓ cup whipping cream

¾ cup tawny port

10 to 12 ounces strawberries, rinsed, hulled, and dried

2 large ripe bananas

4 slices fresh pineapple, about ¾ inch thick and cored

6 slices pound cake (Brown Butter Pound Cake, page 34, or store-bought), about ¾ inch thick

Combine the chocolate and cream in the top of a double boiler and melt over medium heat, stirring often. When fully melted and smooth, stir in the port. Keep warm over low heat until you are ready to serve.

Halve or quarter large strawberries; leave smaller berries whole. Cut the bananas into ½-inch-thick slices on the bias. Cut the pineapple slices and pound cake slices into strips about ¾ inch thick.

Arrange the fruit and cake on a plate or platter. Pour the warm fondue mixture into butter warmer dishes and set them in their stands, having your guests light the tea candles once they are at their seats. Or simply serve the fondue mixture in ramekins or other small dishes.

MAKES 6 FONDUES

▲ Double all the ingredients, especially if you are using ramekins or other dishes for serving.

▼ Halve all the ingredients.

☺ Prepare the chocolate mixture up to 4 hours ahead and gently reheat before serving. Prepare the fruit 1 hour ahead and lay damp paper towels on top to keep moist and fresh; dip banana slices in orange juice to keep from browning as on page 106.

2

SKEWERS

AND PICKS

One of the simplest ways to turn "regular" food into finger food
is to spear it on a skewer or pierce it with a toothpick. And it
seems rather dainty, doesn't it, lifting the tip of a pick and deftly
dropping a morsel in your mouth? Game night wouldn't be quite
the same without this versatile category. The recipes that follow
include both snack-size bites that are ideal to kick off the evening,
as well as some more substantial preparations.

Pickled Grape and Blue Cheese Skewers

They may be small picks, barely a mouthful, but they pack a good punch of flavor with quick-pickled grapes and robust blue cheese. Be sure to use a thinner toothpick-style pick for these little skewers. Larger skewers can split the cubes of cheese.

1 cup water

¾ cup red wine vinegar

1 teaspoon coriander seeds

1 teaspoon mustard seeds

1 teaspoon allspice berries

5 whole cloves

2 bay leaves (preferably fresh), lightly torn

24 large red seedless grapes

4 ounces blue cheese, cut into 24 cubes

Combine the water, vinegar, coriander seeds, mustard seeds, allspice, cloves, and bay leaves in a small saucepan. Bring just to a boil, then reduce the heat to medium-low and simmer for 1 minute. Put the grapes in a heatproof bowl and add the warm pickling mixture. Let cool, then cover and refrigerate for at least 2 hours.

When you are ready to serve, drain the grapes and dry on paper towels. Spear a pickled grape and a cube of cheese onto the end of small decorative picks. The snacks will stand upright if you don't fully pierce the cheese cube. Arrange them on a platter or tray and serve.

MAKES 24 SMALL SKEWERS

▲ Double or triple all the ingredients.
▼ Halve all the ingredients.
☺ Pickle the grapes up to 1 day ahead, though they will become more strongly flavored. Assemble the skewers up to 2 hours before serving, cover loosely with plastic wrap, and refrigerate; let come to room temperature before serving.

Grilled Garlicky Mushrooms

To echo a classic steakhouse side dish, you might consider serving these with the Peppered Steak with Balsamic Red Onions (page 49). After all, the grill's already going, so you might as well take advantage of it. Try to choose mushrooms of an even size, ideally with caps about 1½ inches across.

If you don't want to grill, you can broil the mushrooms instead, arranging them on a rimmed baking sheet and broiling them until tender, turning them once halfway through. In this case you won't need to skewer the mushrooms for cooking, just slip them onto picks for serving.

....

¼ cup dry white wine or dry vermouth

¼ cup olive oil

1 tablespoon minced or pressed garlic

1 teaspoon minced fresh thyme

Salt and freshly ground black pepper

18 to 20 mushrooms (about 1 pound), stems trimmed to cap level

Stir together the wine, olive oil, garlic, and thyme in a large bowl and add a good pinch each of salt and pepper. Add the mushrooms and stir well to evenly coat in the garlic mixture. Set aside for 30 to 60 minutes, stirring occasionally. The mushrooms will absorb most of the liquid in this time. Soak 8 (6-inch) bamboo skewers in water for at least 1 hour.

Preheat an outdoor grill. Thread the mushrooms onto the skewers horizontally through the cap (with the stem on one side), 3 to 4 per skewer. Dense mushrooms can sometimes split when skewered; it helps a bit to rotate the skewer back and forth as you go.

Grill the skewers until the mushrooms are tender, turning once or twice, 8 to 10 minutes. Slip the mushrooms off the skewers and rethread each into a small individual pick. Arrange the mushrooms on a platter and serve, setting the platter on a warming tray to keep warm, if you like.

MAKES 18 TO 20 MUSHROOMS

▲ Double all the ingredients.
▼ Halve the number of mushrooms but make full amount of marinade to assure enough for fully coating the mushrooms.
▲ Marinate and skewer the mushrooms up to 2 hours ahead; grill shortly before serving.

Wasabi Pea–Crusted Tuna

This recipe makes snack-size bites, little morsels of slightly spicy tuna that can be part of the early evening nibbles. Or for two or three players, it can be served in larger portions of more skewers per person

I've used fresh albacore and fresh ahi tuna for this recipe; both are equally delicious. Salmon is a good candidate as well. Wasabi peas are a Japanese snack of dried green peas with a spicy wasabi coating. Look for them where you find other Asian specialty foods. Of course, there's hardly a better game to play when you're serving this than Wasabi!

10 ounces albacore or ahi tuna, cut into 36 cubes

2 tablespoons water

2 teaspoons wasabi powder

$\frac{1}{2}$ teaspoon salt

2 teaspoons Asian sesame oil

$\frac{1}{2}$ cup wasabi peas

2 tablespoons olive oil, plus more if needed

Put the tuna in a bowl. In a separate small bowl, stir together the water, wasabi powder, and salt to make a smooth paste. Stir in the sesame oil, pour the mixture over the tuna, and toss well to evenly mix. Set aside.

Very finely chop the wasabi peas in a food processor and spread them out on a plate.

Thread 6 tuna cubes onto 6-inch skewers in 2 snug groupings of 3 cubes each, with a 1-inch gap between them. Use heavy kitchen shears or the base of a heavy knife to cut the skewer in half. Lightly roll each tuna skewer in the wasabi pea crumbs, patting to remove excess.

Heat the olive oil in a large skillet, preferably nonstick, over medium-high heat. Add the tuna skewers in batches, turning to lightly brown on all sides while leaving the center slightly translucent, about 2 minutes total. Transfer the skewers to a plate and serve, setting it on a warming tray to keep warm, if you like.

MAKES 12 SMALL SKEWERS

▲ Double or triple all the ingredients.
▼ Halve the ingredients, or serve in larger portions of more skewers per person.
☺ Thread and coat the tuna up to 1 hour ahead, cover, and refrigerate; cook just before serving.

Pork Saltimbocca

A traditional Italian entrée charading as a game-friendly snack, these are small, versatile bites. The nibbles can be part of a spread for a group or a good option for a twosome, each person getting eight of the small rolls.

Pork tenderloins often weigh in the 1-pound range, but the narrow tapered end doesn't work well here. That trimmed portion can be used in a number of ways, such as dicing it and adding it to chili or sautéing it to use in a fried rice recipe.

9 ounces pork tenderloin

Salt and freshly ground black pepper

16 sage leaves

2 ounces fontina cheese, thinly sliced

2 ounces thinly sliced prosciutto, cut into 1-inch strips

Preheat the oven to 450°F.

Cut the tenderloin across into 16 slices about ¼ inch thick. Season the pork lightly with salt and pepper. Top each slice with a sage leaf and piece of fontina (trimmed to fit the shape of the meat) and roll the slice up into a snug roll. Wrap a strip of prosciutto around the outside and spear the roll onto a small bamboo pick or skewer.

Arrange the pork rolls on a rimmed baking sheet and bake until no longer pink in the center, 6 to 8 minutes (no turning needed). Transfer the rolls to a plate to serve, setting it on a warming tray to keep warm, if you wish.

MAKES 16 ROLLS

▲ Double or triple all the ingredients.

▼ It is hard to halve, but you can serve larger portions of more skewers per person.

☺ Prepare the rolls up to 4 hours ahead, cover, and refrigerate. This is best baked shortly before serving.

Herb-Marinated Shrimp

This is a quick recipe to whip together. After just an hour of marinating—during which time you're conserving energy for a raucous evening of game play—you'll be getting raves from guests! The flavors will be best if you use at least three different types of herbs. The onions I use here are the same as the ones used for cocktails. Gibson anyone?

$1/2$ cup chopped fresh tender herbs (flat-leaf parsley, tarragon, fennel, chervil, and/or chives)

$1/4$ cup white wine vinegar

$1/4$ cup olive oil

Salt and freshly ground black pepper

18 extra-large shrimp (about 1 pound), peeled and deveined

18 pickled cocktail onions

Combine the herbs, vinegar, and olive oil, with a good pinch each of salt and pepper in a bowl. Stir to mix; set aside.

Bring a pan of salted water to a boil. Add the shrimp and cook until just opaque through the thickest part, about 2 minutes. Drain well and let cool for a few minutes. Add the warm shrimp to the marinade and let cool to room temperature, stirring a few times. Cover and refrigerate until chilled, at least 1 hour, stirring occasionally.

To serve, spear each shrimp onto a small skewer or pick, with 1 pickled onion in the nook of the shrimp's curve. It's fine for some of the herbs to be clinging to the shrimp, but brush off the excessive herbs. Arrange the shrimp skewers on a plate and serve.

MAKES 18 SMALL SKEWERS

▲ Double or triple all the ingredients, but use no more than 1 cup chopped herbs.

▼ Halve all the ingredients.

☺ Marinate the shrimp up to 8 hours ahead. Assemble the skewers up to 2 hours ahead, arrange on plate, cover with plastic wrap, and refrigerate until you are ready to serve.

Swordfish and Fennel Skewers

You might feel a bit too old to be playing Go Fish, but with this recipe you can just "go swordfish" instead and stick to the game of Taboo you had planned. Or, if you prefer, you can substitute another firm, meaty fish like salmon or tuna.

1 medium fennel bulb

3 tablespoons dry white wine

3 tablespoons olive oil

$\frac{1}{2}$ teaspoon fennel seeds, crushed

Salt and freshly ground black pepper

$1\frac{1}{4}$ pounds swordfish steak, skin removed, cut into 24 cubes

Trim the stalks from the fennel bulb, reserving the tender green fronds. Cut the tough base from the bulb, then halve it vertically. Cut out and discard the core and separate the layers. Cut the bulb pieces into roughly $\frac{3}{4}$-inch squares. Finely chop enough of the fennel fronds to make 2 tablespoons.

Combine the wine, olive oil, fennel seeds, chopped fennel, and a good pinch each of salt and pepper in a medium bowl. Stir to mix, then add the swordfish, stirring gently to evenly coat the fish. Refrigerate for 1 hour, stirring once or twice. Soak 12 (6-inch) bamboo skewers or sturdy picks in cold water for at least 1 hour.

When you are ready to cook the fish, preheat an outdoor grill or the broiler. Thread 2 swordfish cubes onto each skewer, alternating with pieces of fennel bulb. Grill or broil the fish until it is just opaque through, 5 to 7 minutes, turning the skewers once or twice.

Transfer the grilled skewers to a platter and serve; set on a warming tray to keep warm, if you wish.

MAKES 12 SKEWERS

▲ Double or triple all the ingredients.

▼ Halve all the ingredients.

☺ Marinate the fish up to 4 hours ahead, refrigerated. Assemble the skewers and grill them shortly before serving.

Spicy Meatballs with Yogurt-Cucumber Dip

This recipe brought to mind the Score Four game I played so much as a kid but haven't thought about in ages. Balls of pale and dark wood are dropped onto pegs on a four-by-four grid of vertical pegs. Players work to make a tic-tac-toe–like series of their color going vertically, horizontally, or diagonally. If I was really motivated, I'd re-create a Score Four board using this recipe and another batch made with paler ground veal. One of these days.

You can use any hot sauce that you like for spicing up the meatballs; harissa is a great option, too. Better to start with just a small amount and add more to taste, rather than overdo it up front. I recommend cooking a sample of the meat mixture to check for seasoning before cooking all the meatballs.

YOGURT-CUCUMBER DIP

1/2 cucumber, peeled, seeded, and diced (about 1 cup)

1/2 teaspoon salt, plus more as needed

3/4 cup plain whole-milk yogurt

MEATBALLS

1 pound lean ground beef

1/2 pound lean ground pork

1/2 cup finely minced onion

3 cloves garlic, minced or pressed

1 tablespoon Sriracha or other hot sauce, plus more to taste

1 1/2 teaspoons dried thyme

Salt

2 tablespoons vegetable oil

To make the dip, toss the cucumber with 1/2 teaspoon of the salt and set aside for 30 minutes. Rinse, drain well, and pat dry with paper towels. Combine the cucumber and yogurt in a food processor and purée until nearly smooth. Transfer to a medium serving bowl and taste for seasoning, adding more salt to taste. Cover and refrigerate until you are ready to serve.

To make the meatballs, combine the ground beef, ground pork, onion, garlic, Sriracha, thyme, and a good pinch of salt in a bowl. Mix with your hands until thoroughly blended. Cook up about 1 teaspoon of the mixture in a small skillet with a bit of oil and taste for seasoning. Add more hot sauce or salt to taste. Form the mixture into 1-inch balls.

Preheat the oven to 250°F.

Heat the oil in a large skillet over medium heat. Add half of the meatballs and cook until lightly browned on all sides and no longer pink in the center, about 10 minutes, turning often to cook evenly. (The meatballs should not crowd the skillet. Cook in three batches if needed.) Set aside on a paper towel–lined baking sheet and repeat with the remaining meatballs. Keep the meatballs warm in the oven until you are ready to serve (up to 30 minutes).

Skewer 1 meatball each on small picks or decorative tooth-picks and arrange them on a platter for serving; set on a warming tray to keep warm, if you wish. Pour the dip into individual bowls or dishes and set them alongside.

MAKES ABOUT 36 MEATBALLS WITH DIP

▲ Double all the ingredients.

▼ Halve all the ingredients. Or spear 2 to 3 meatballs per pick for larger portions.

☺ Cook the meatballs up to 1 day ahead, wrap well in aluminum foil, and refriger-ate. Reheat in a 250°F oven, wrapped to keep moist. Make the dip up to 1 day ahead, cover, and refrigerate.

FOR GAME LOVERS: *GAMES* MAGAZINE

My husband and I are longtime subscribers to *Games* magazine (gamesmagazine-online.com); he first started reading it back in the 1970s shortly after it began pub-lication. Each issue is packed with word puzzles, brain teasers, and other games. They also publish articles about game creators, game history, quirky game novelties, game reviews, tournaments, anything relating to the world of games. Each December issue features their annual list of "games of the year," in categories that include party games, puzzles, family games, strategy games, and others of the "traditional (non-electronic)" genre. (They give awards for electronic games, too.) The 2009 winner in the New Party Game category was Go Nuts! Other recent winners in the category include GiftTrap, Wits & Wagers, Snorta, and Cranium Hoopla. Check out, also, their Hall of Fame, whose most recent inductee was Settlers of Catan.

Lamb and Olive Kebabs

Inspired by the traditional flavors of a Moroccan tagine, these small kebabs are packed with robust character—just the thing to add some spice to your evening's games, which may manifest in a boisterous charades performance or a daring Stratego strategy. You can broil the skewers as well, 3 to 4 minutes per side.

1 lemon

24 large pitted green olives (can be pimento-stuffed)

1½ teaspoons ground cumin

1½ teaspoons ground coriander

1 teaspoon ground ginger

1 teaspoon ground turmeric

1 teaspoon sweet Hungarian paprika

1 teaspoon salt

¼ teaspoon freshly ground black pepper

⅓ cup olive oil

1 pound boneless lamb sirloin, trimmed and cut into 24 cubes

Peel strips of zest from the lemon and set aside. Squeeze the juice and put it in a small bowl. Add the olives and toss to coat. Set aside while you prepare the kebabs, stirring occasionally.

Combine the cumin, coriander, ginger, turmeric, paprika, salt, and pepper in a bowl. Stir to evenly mix, then stir in the olive oil and lemon zest. Add the lamb pieces, stir to coat, and refrigerate for at least 2 hours, stirring occasionally. Soak 12 (6-inch) bamboo skewers in cold water for at least 1 hour.

Preheat an outdoor grill. Thread 2 lamb cubes and 2 olives, alternating, onto one end of each skewer. Grill until the lamb is lightly pink in the center, 5 to 7 minutes, turning once. Arrange the skewers on a platter and serve; set on a warming tray to keep warm, if you wish.

MAKES 12 SKEWERS

▲ Double or triple all the ingredients.

▼ Halve the ingredients or serve 3 or 4 skewers per person.

☺ Marinate the meat up to 6 hours ahead; assemble the skewers and grill them just before serving.

SOAKING SKEWERS

Soaking is the best defense against the exposed woody ends of a bamboo skewer burning while on the grill—the wet wood may brown a bit but is less likely to fully burn. Although it might seem more convenient to assemble skewers an hour or two before grilling, the ends can dry out again before you toss them on the grill and the risk of burning will be greater. It's not a major safety issue, just one of aesthetics and ease of eating. The perfect solution would be slender 4- to 6-inch metal skewers, but like a royal flush in my poker hand, these have eluded me thus far.

Peppered Steak with Balsamic Red Onions

A classic, perennial combination comes to life in game-friendly form: grilled steak and onions. All you need now is a pitcher of Manhattans (page 130), a potato with the works (page 68, in bite-sized form), and your best poker buddies. Sounds like the perfect game night to me!

1 red onion, cut into 1-inch slices

¼ cup balsamic vinegar

2 tablespoons olive oil

1¼ pounds sirloin or tri-tip steak, cut into 24 cubes

1½ teaspoons coarsely ground black pepper

1 teaspoon sweet Hungarian paprika

½ teaspoon salt

Separate the rings of the onion slices and cut them into 1-inch pieces, saving the smaller centers of the rings for another use. You'll want 4 to 5 dozen onion pieces. Toss together the onion, vinegar, and 1 tablespoon of the olive oil in a bowl. Set aside for 1 hour, stirring occasionally. Soak 12 (6-inch) bamboo skewers in cold water for at least 1 hour.

Put the steak cubes in a bowl. Add the remaining 1 table-spoon of the olive oil, the pepper, paprika, and salt. Toss with your hands, rubbing the meat pieces well to be sure they're evenly coated with the seasonings. Set aside while heating the grill. (Refrigerate if the kitchen's quite warm or if you are preparing the meat more than 1 hour in advance.)

Preheat an outdoor grill. Thread 2 beef pieces onto one end of each skewer, with 4 or 5 onion pieces between them. Grill (keeping the empty skewer ends away from the heat as much as possible) until the beef is nicely browned and medium-rare in the center, 2 to 3 minutes per side. Transfer to a platter to serve; set on a warming tray to keep warm, if you wish.

MAKES 12 SKEWERS

▲ Double or triple all the ingredients.
▼ Halve all the ingredients.
☺ Marinate the steak up to 6 hours ahead; marinate the onions up to 2 hours ahead. Assemble the skewers and grill them shortly before serving.

Beef Yakitori

Like the Tripoley and cribbage we used to play so often together, yakitori is something of a tradition in my family. Dad's navy career had us living in Japan for a few years (I was born there), and just outside the gates of the base was a small yakitori restaurant my parents often patronized. This recipe is based on one my mom came home with from Japan. These flavorful skewers can be made with chicken in place of beef, if you wish. I recommend using boneless, skinless chicken thighs; they remain more tender and juicy on the grill than does chicken breast meat.

TERIYAKI MARINADE

1/2 cup mirin (sweet rice wine) or dry sherry

1/2 cup soy sauce, preferably reduced-sodium

1/2 cup chicken broth

1 tablespoon finely grated or minced fresh ginger

1 teaspoon pressed or minced garlic

3/4 pound sirloin or tri-tip steak

8 green onions, trimmed to 4 inches from root end

2 teaspoons toasted sesame seeds

To make the marinade, combine the mirin, soy sauce, chicken broth, ginger, and garlic in a small saucepan. Bring to a boil and simmer for 1 minute. Pour the marinade into a shallow dish large enough to hold the meat and set aside to cool.

Cut the beef into 24 (1-inch) squares about 1/2 inch thick. Add the beef to the cooled marinade, stir to evenly coat, and refrigerate for at least 1 hour, stirring occasionally. Cut the trimmed green onions into thirds. Soak 12 (4- to 6-inch) bamboo skewers in water for at least 1 hour.

Preheat an outdoor grill.

Thread 2 pieces of beef and green onion, alternating, onto one end of each skewer. Grill the skewers until the meat is nicely browned and just a bit pink in the center, about 2 minutes per side. Transfer the skewers to a plate or small platter and sprinkle with the sesame seeds. Set the plate on a warming tray to keep warm, if you wish.

MAKES 12 SKEWERS

▲ Double or triple all the ingredients.

▼ Halve the ingredients, or serve larger portions of more skewers per person.

☾ Marinate the beef for up to 8 hours, refrigerated. It is best to skewer the meat and grill just before serving.

Mole Flank Steak with Pickled Peppers

With all due respect to the classic and elaborate moles from the Oaxaca region of Mexico, this is indeed a quick-and-easy variation on the richly flavored sauce. (I may cheat at mole, but I never cheat at cards.) The steak is grilled whole, then sliced to wrap around pickled peppers for a small bite that's packed with flavor. These are plenty tasty at room temperature.

¼ cup finely chopped onion

2 tablespoons top-quality unsweetened cocoa powder

1 tablespoon ancho chile powder

1 tablespoon sesame seeds

1 teaspoon chipotle chile powder

1 teaspoon minced or pressed garlic

2 tablespoons olive oil

2 tablespoons water

½ teaspoon salt

1 flank steak (about 1¼ pounds)

25 to 30 pickled peppers, such as pepperoncini or sport peppers

Combine the onion, cocoa powder, ancho chile powder, sesame seeds, chipotle chile powder, and garlic in a food processor (a mini processor, if you have one) and process until smooth. Add the olive oil, water, and salt and pulse to evenly blend.

Lightly score both sides of the flank steak in a diamond pattern with the tip of a small knife. Rub the cocoa mixture evenly over both sides of the steak, wrap in plastic, and refrigerate for at least 1 hour.

Preheat an outdoor grill. Grill the steak until medium, 3 to 4 minutes per side. Transfer to a chopping board and let sit for 5 minutes. Cut the steak across the grain, at a slight angle, into ½-inch-thick slices. Cut longer slices crosswise in half, so the pieces are about 3 to 4 inches long.

Working on a double thickness of paper towel to help contain the liquids, cut the stem end from each pickled pepper, emptying the juices from the interior. (This makes for much tidier eating later.) Any large peppers should be halved lengthwise.

Wrap a piece of flank steak around a pepper and skewer it at the end of a 6-inch bamboo skewer, then add another steak-wrapped pepper, so there are two pieces at the end of the skewer. Repeat with the remaining steak and peppers. Arrange the skewers on a platter, or upright in a bowl filled with rock salt.

MAKES 12 TO 15 SKEWERS

▲ Double all the ingredients, grilling the steaks side by side.

▼ Hard to halve.

☺ Marinate the steak up to 6 hours ahead and refrigerate; grill the meat and assemble the skewers shortly before serving.

3 ALL-EDIBLES

This class of recipes represents the game-night host's very best friends. These dishes pass not only the clean-fingers test, but the clean-kitchen test as well. You'll just need trays or platters for serving, no small dishes or skewers or other eating implements. The recipes take advantage of foods that are inherently good serving pieces—from sliced daikon radish to mini biscuits—on (or in) which savory and sweet mixtures sit. One hundred percent edible, they won't contribute any dishes to after-party cleanup, which is the bonus. And all-edibles are inherently pop-in-your-mouth gratifying to eat!

Aged Cheddar with Dried Cherry–Almond Chutney

This will take you on a trip in the way-back machine: remember Hi Ho Cherry-O? It was, for many of us, one of the first counting games we played. Here the only counting you'll have to do is counting on how much your friends are going to love this combination of nutty aged cheese and nut-embellished cherry chutney. You can use chopped dried apricots or dried cranberries in place of the cherries for a different take on the chutney.

DRIED CHERRY–ALMOND CHUTNEY

4 ounces dried sour cherries, chopped (about ¾ cup)

3 tablespoons red wine vinegar

1 tablespoon olive oil

¼ cup minced red onion

2 tablespoons honey

⅓ cup toasted slivered almonds (see page 9)

24 baguette slices

8 ounces aged cheddar or other aged cheese (such as Gouda or Gruyère), cut into ¼-inch slices

To make the chutney, put the dried cherries and vinegar in a small bowl. Add hot tap water to just cover the cherries and set aside to plump for about 30 minutes.

Heat the olive oil in a small skillet over medium heat. Add the onion and cook, stirring, until tender and aromatic, 1 to 2 minutes. Add the cherries with their liquid and the honey, and cook until most of the liquid has evaporated, 8 to 10 minutes. Set aside to cool.

When you are ready to serve, top the baguette slices with the aged cheddar cheese, trimming the cheese into smaller portions as needed to fit on the bread. Stir the toasted almonds into the chutney and spoon a dollop on top of each cheese slice. Arrange the baguette slices on a platter or tray and serve.

MAKES 24 PIECES

▲ Double all the ingredients.

▼ Halve the cheese and number of baguette slices. Save any extra chutney for another use.

☺ Make the chutney up to 1 week ahead, cover, and refrigerate. Stir in the almonds and assemble up to 1 hour before serving.

Artichoke-Stuffed Mushrooms

This retro classic weaves in and out of style but never loses its popularity. Of the countless stuffing options—from simple herbed bread crumbs to rich meat—I love this unfussy blend with finely chopped artichoke hearts.

24 large mushrooms (about 1½ pounds)

2 tablespoons olive oil

½ cup finely chopped tomato

1 (14-ounce) can quartered artichoke hearts, rinsed and well drained

⅓ cup dried bread crumbs

¼ cup fresh finely grated Parmesan cheese

¼ cup finely grated fontina cheese

Salt and freshly ground black pepper

Snap off the stems from the mushroom caps, leaving a natural cavity for stuffing. If the stem breaks off before the spot where it meets the cap, scoop out the rest with a small spoon. Reserve the stems. Set the mushrooms cavity side up in a baking dish and set aside.

Preheat the oven to 400°F.

Put the mushroom stems in a food processor and pulse to finely chop. Heat the olive oil in a large skillet over medium heat. Add the mushroom stems to the skillet (reserve the processor bowl) with the tomato and cook, stirring occasionally, until tender and most of the liquid has evaporated, about 5 minutes. Meanwhile, put the artichoke hearts in the food processor and pulse to finely chop. Add the artichoke hearts to the skillet and cook for 1 minute longer. Set the pan aside to cool. Stir in the bread crumbs and cheeses, then season the mixture to taste with salt and pepper.

Spoon about 1 tablespoon of the filling into each mushroom cap, mounding it slightly (it's easiest to do this with your fingers, pressing the stuffing well into the cavity).

Bake until the mushrooms are just tender, about 25 minutes. Set aside to cool slightly. Transfer the mushrooms to a platter for serving; set on a warming tray to keep warm, if you wish.

MAKES 24 STUFFED MUSHROOMS

▲ Double all the ingredients; bake on a rimmed baking sheet or in 2 baking pans.

▼ Halve all the ingredients.

☺ Stuff the mushrooms up to 6 hours ahead, cover, and refrigerate. These are best baked shortly before serving, adding about 5 minutes to the baking time if direct from the refrigerator.

Mini Tostadas with Cumin Black Beans

Taking favorite tostada or taco combinations down to a mini, one-bite form is a simple idea that is open to many variations. You can replace some or all of the beans with cooked ground beef, minced leftover chicken, or chorizo. Add fresh chiles for extra flavor.

Tostitos brand "Scoops" chips, small cups of thin crisp tortilla, are ideal for bite-sized portions. Otherwise you can use round tortilla chips, choosing the flattest from the bag. Since the chips will lose some of their bright crunch after an hour or so, it's best to assemble the tostadas shortly before serving.

1 tablespoon olive oil

½ cup minced onion

1 teaspoon minced or pressed garlic

1½ teaspoons ground cumin

1 cup finely chopped tomato

1 (15-ounce) can black beans, rinsed and drained

Salt and freshly ground black pepper

½ cup finely diced avocado

3 tablespoons chopped fresh cilantro

2 tablespoons freshly squeezed lime juice

36 tortilla chips (cups or rounds)

¼ cup sour cream

½ cup grated sharp cheddar cheese

Heat the oil in a skillet over medium heat. Add the onion and garlic and cook until beginning to soften, 2 to 3 minutes. Stir in the cumin and cook, stirring, until it evenly coats the onion and smells aromatic, about 1 minute. Add the tomato and black beans and cook, stirring occasionally, until the mixture has thickened slightly, 5 to 7 minutes. Season to taste with salt and pepper, then set aside to cool.

Stir the avocado, cilantro, and lime juice into the black bean mixture. Spoon the mixture onto the chips and top each with a small dollop of sour cream and a pinch of grated cheese. Arrange the tortilla chips on a platter and serve.

MAKES 36 TOSTADAS

▲ Double all the ingredients.

▼ Halve all the ingredients.

☺ Make the filling up to 4 hours ahead, cover, and refrigerate, letting it come to room temperature before assembling. Assemble just before serving.

Tuna Tartare on Daikon Slices

Ginger—in both fresh and pickled forms—adds a bright, peppery contrast to the rich raw tuna in this tartare. If your grocery store sells sushi, look for pickled ginger in that vicinity or in the Asian section. Otherwise check Asian or specialty food markets. Daikon, a large white variety of mild radish, slices up into crisp rounds, ideal for serving the tartare. You can use slices of cucumber instead. Ginger juice is very easy to make: finely grate about $1\frac{1}{2}$ teaspoons of ginger and press it in a sieve with the back of a spoon to release the juice.

6 ounces sashimi-grade tuna, cut into $\frac{1}{4}$-inch dice

3 tablespoons thinly sliced green onion, white and pale green portions

2 tablespoons finely chopped pickled ginger

1 tablespoon freshly squeezed lemon juice

1 tablespoon olive oil

$\frac{1}{2}$ teaspoon fresh ginger juice (see above)

Salt and freshly ground black pepper

24 ($\frac{1}{4}$-inch) slices daikon radish

Radish sprouts, for garnish (optional)

Combine the tuna, green onion, pickled ginger, lemon juice, olive oil, and ginger juice in a bowl. Toss well and season lightly with salt and pepper. Refrigerate until you are ready to serve.

Shortly before serving, spoon the tuna tartare onto the daikon slices and arrange them on a platter or tray. Top with a few radish sprouts and serve.

MAKES 24 MINI TARTARES

▲ Double or triple all the ingredients.

▼ Halve all the ingredients.

☺ Make the tartare up to 4 hours ahead, cover, and refrigerate. Assemble up to 1 hour ahead, cover with plastic wrap, and refrigerate.

GASTRO GAMES: WASABI! (Z-Man Games, 2008)

Warning: This game *will* make you want to go out for a rainbow roll and some himachi after you play. It did to me the first time I had a go at Wasabi! Pick ingredient tiles from the pantry (most of the sushi standards, from cucumber to sea urchin) and lay them, alternating with your play mates, on the game board. You're working to complete sushi combos based on recipe cards you've drawn. It's a pretty simple premise, though the game can take a few twists and turns thanks to a little strategy and those prized special cards players earn after showing solid sushi-making skills.

Herbed Biscuits with Smoked Salmon

Tender cold-smoked salmon is my first choice here; other cold-smoked fish, such as sturgeon, can be used as well. If you'd like to use hot-smoked fish instead (also delicious), coarsely flake it, removing any skin and bones as you go. Stir it into the crème fraîche and lemon zest, then spoon the mixture onto the biscuits.

HERBED BISCUITS

2 cups all-purpose flour

1 tablespoon baking powder

$1/2$ teaspoon salt

$1/2$ cup unsalted butter, cut into pieces and chilled

$3/4$ cup whole milk

2 tablespoons minced green onion, white and pale green portions

2 tablespoons minced fresh chives

2 tablespoons minced fresh flat-leaf parsley

8 ounces cold-smoked salmon, thinly sliced

$3/4$ cup crème fraîche or sour cream

2 teaspoons finely grated lemon zest

Preheat the oven to 400°F. Line a baking sheet with a silicone baking mat or parchment paper.

To make the biscuits, combine the flour, baking powder, and salt in a food processor and pulse once or twice to blend. Add the butter and pulse until it is finely chopped and the mixture has the texture of coarse cornmeal. Transfer the mixture to a bowl and add the milk, green onion, chives, and parsley. Gently stir until the dough is evenly mixed; avoid overmixing.

Transfer the biscuit dough to a lightly floured work surface. Press the dough into a 9-inch square about $1/2$ inch thick. Cut the dough into 6 even strips in each direction, making 36 squares. Set the biscuits on the baking sheet about 1 inch apart. Bake until puffed and lightly browned, 12 to 15 minutes. Transfer the biscuits to a wire rack to cool.

Cut each biscuit in half horizontally. Cut the smoked salmon into strips about 1 inch wide and a few inches long. Stir together the crème fraîche and lemon zest in a small bowl.

To assemble the biscuits, fold the salmon strips into 1-inch squares and set them on the bottom portions of the biscuits, add a dollop of the crème fraîche, and top with the other biscuit halves. Arrange the biscuits on a platter or tray and serve.

MAKES 36 BISCUITS

▲ Double all the ingredients, making the biscuits in batches.

▼ Best not to halve, but you can cut the biscuits into 16 pieces for larger portions.

☺ Make the biscuits 1 day ahead and store in airtight container; split and fill not more than 1 hour before serving.

Salmon Poke in Endive Leaves

Salmon may not be a traditional ingredient in Hawaii, where the classic raw preparation of *poke* (poh-kay) is applied to many types of seafood. But using salmon suits my Northwestern roots, and it shines in the poke style. Feel free to substitute the more traditional ahi tuna, if you wish.

....

$\frac{3}{4}$ pound previously frozen salmon fillet, skin and pin bones removed

$\frac{1}{2}$ cup thinly sliced red onion

$\frac{1}{4}$ cup moderately packed fresh cilantro leaves

2 tablespoons soy sauce

1 tablespoon Asian sesame oil

$\frac{1}{4}$ teaspoon Sriracha or other hot pepper sauce, more to taste

4 to 5 heads Belgian endive, trimmed

Cut the salmon into $\frac{1}{4}$-inch cubes and put it in a bowl with the red onion and cilantro leaves. Stir together the soy sauce, sesame oil, and Sriracha sauce in a small dish. Pour this over the salmon and toss gently. Set aside for 10 to 15 minutes, stirring once or twice.

Discard any torn or damaged outer leaves from the endive. Remove leaves that are at least 3 inches long and set aside for serving; you'll need 24 in all. Save the smaller leaves at the core for another use (such as sliced to add to a salad).

To serve, spoon the salmon poke into the broad end of the endive leaves and arrange them on a platter.

MAKES 24 LEAVES

▲ Double or triple all the ingredients.

▼ Halve all the ingredients.

☺ Make the salmon up to 4 hours ahead, cover, and refrigerate; the flavors develop more the longer it sits. Assemble in the endive up to 1 hour ahead, cover with lightly dampened paper towels to keep moist, and refrigerate.

Polenta Squares with Spicy Sausage and Spinach

This filling is on the hot side, so start with just ¼ teaspoon of the hot red pepper flakes if you prefer less heat. These polenta squares can be filled with any number of mixtures, perhaps even the kale and ricotta filling from the pasta shells on page 64. Just be sure that your filling is cohesive enough to hold its shape in the shallow indentation of the polenta.

POLENTA

3 cups water

1 teaspoon salt

¾ cup coarse polenta

½ cup freshly grated Parmesan cheese

¾ teaspoon minced fresh oregano, or ½ teaspoon dried

FILLING

¼ pound bulk pork sausage meat (unseasoned or just lightly seasoned)

½ teaspoon fennel seeds

½ teaspoon dried red pepper flakes

3 cups packed fresh spinach leaves (about 4 ounces), coarsely chopped

¾ cup whole-milk ricotta cheese

Salt

To make the polenta, bring the water and salt to a boil in a saucepan. Gradually whisk in the polenta and when all has been added, reduce the heat to medium-low. Continue cooking until the polenta is thickened and tender to the bite, about 20 minutes, whisking occasionally at the beginning, more regularly toward the end. Take the pan from the heat and whisk in the Parmesan cheese and oregano. Transfer the polenta to a lightly oiled 9-inch square pan and smooth the top. Let sit for about 15 minutes.

When the polenta is partially set but still warm, use the tip of a knife to score the polenta into 12 portions: 3 strips in one direction, 4 strips in the other. Find a spice or condiment jar on your shelves, or a shot glass, that has about a 1¼-inch base. Clean and lightly oil the bottom of the jar and use it to press an indentation about ½ inch deep in the center of each polenta portion. Cover and refrigerate the polenta until fully chilled.

To make the filling, cook the sausage in a skillet over medium heat until no longer pink in the center, 5 to 7 minutes, breaking up the sausage into small pieces as it cooks. Drain off any excess fat, then add the fennel seeds and red pepper flakes, cooking until the spices are aromatic, about 1 minute. Add the spinach and cook, stirring, until wilted, about 1 minute. Set aside to cool for 10 minutes. Drain away any liquid that may have accumulated, then stir in the ricotta. Season to taste with salt.

Preheat the oven to 375°F. Line a baking sheet with parchment paper or lightly oiled foil.

Cut the polenta where it was scored and transfer the pieces to the baking sheet. Spoon the sausage-spinach filling into the indentation on each piece of polenta, mounding it slightly. Bake until heated through, 10 to 12 minutes. Transfer to a platter and serve; set on a warming tray to keep warm, if you wish.

MAKES 12 SQUARES

▲ Double all the ingredients, forming the polenta squares in 2 pans.

▼ Best not to halve.

☺ Make the polenta squares and filling up to 1 day ahead. Store the polenta, well-wrapped, and the filling, covered, in the refrigerator. Fill and arrange on a baking sheet up to 2 hours ahead and refrigerate; bake shortly before serving, adding about 5 minutes to the baking time if direct from the refrigerator.

Stuffed Large Pasta Shells with Kale-Ricotta Filling

This game-friendly pasta dish has traditional lasagna elements in small, bite-sized packages. When choosing kale, I usually opt for the Lacinato variety, with its deep green, bumpy-looking leaves and vivid flavor. Other types of kale work well, too. The tomato sauce should be on the thin side, not too chunky; whirl yours in a food processor or blender if needed.

24 jumbo pasta shells

1 bunch (about ¾ pound) kale

1 tablespoon olive oil

2 ounces pancetta or thick-cut bacon, diced

1 cup finely chopped onion

3 cloves garlic, minced or pressed

1 teaspoon minced fresh oregano, or ½ teaspoon dried

Salt and freshly ground black pepper

1 (15-ounce) container whole-milk ricotta cheese

⅓ cup finely grated Parmesan cheese

3 tablespoons finely chopped sun-dried tomatoes (oil-packed or plumped dried)

¾ cup tomato sauce (page 95 or store-bought)

Bring a large pan of salted water to a rolling boil. Add the pasta shells and cook, stirring occasionally, until nearly al dente (a bit undercooked), 8 to 10 minutes. Drain well, rinse under cold water to cool, and lay the shells out on paper towels to drain; avoid having them touch, to avoid sticking. Let cool.

Trim the tough stems from the kale leaves and coarsely chop the kale. Heat the olive oil in a large skillet over medium heat. Add pancetta and cook until lightly browned, 2 to 3 minutes. Add the onion and garlic and cook, stirring occasionally, until tender and aromatic, 3 to 5 minutes. Add the kale and cook, stirring often, until the kale is fully tender and bright green, 5 to 7 minutes. Stir in the oregano with salt and pepper to taste. Transfer the kale mixture to a medium bowl and let cool, then stir in the ricotta, Parmesan, and sun-dried tomatoes.

Preheat the oven to 350°F. Lightly oil a 9 by 13-inch baking dish.

Hold one of the pasta shells in your hand, gently pinching the ends to broaden the opening. Spoon about 1 tablespoon of the kale mixture into the shell and top with a couple teaspoons of the tomato sauce. Set the shell in the baking dish and repeat with the remaining shells. Cover the dish with aluminum foil and bake the shells until heated through, about 25 minutes. Use tongs to transfer the shells to a platter for serving; set on a warming tray to keep warm, if you wish.

MAKES 24 SHELLS

▲ Double all the ingredients and bake in 2 dishes.

▼ Halve all the ingredients.

☺ Stuff the shells up to 5 hours ahead, arrange in the baking dish, cover, and refrigerate; they will be best baked shortly before serving, adding about 5 minutes to the baking time if direct from the refrigerator.

Baby Baja Tacos

Feel free to try other fish in this tasty little taco; salmon and ahi tuna are good candidates. For slightly larger servings, simply halve each taco instead of cutting them into thirds. Those classic frilly toothpicks are ideal for securing the tacos, but other small thin picks can be used instead.

½ cup sour cream

1½ teaspoons finely grated lime zest

1 pound snapper, halibut, or other firm, mild fish fillets, skin and pin bones removed

Salt and freshly ground black pepper

½ cup all-purpose flour

¼ cup peanut or canola oil

6 small (6-inch) flour tortillas

1 cup thinly shredded green cabbage

½ cup moderately packed fresh cilantro leaves

1 plum tomato, halved lengthwise and thinly sliced

Stir together the sour cream and lime zest in a small bowl. Refrigerate until it is needed.

Cut the fish fillets across into strips about ¾ inch wide. (If any of the strips are much thicker than 1½ inches, halve them lengthwise.) Season the fish with salt and pepper, then coat with the flour, patting to remove excess.

Heat the oil in a large skillet, preferably nonstick, over medium-high heat. Add the fish strips and cook until nicely browned and crisp, about 3 minutes per side. If your skillet isn't large enough to hold all the fish without crowding, cook it in 2 batches.

Spread the tortillas with an even, thin layer of the sour cream. Lay pieces of the fish across the center, breaking some into smaller pieces to fill the length of the tortilla if needed. Top the fish with a layer of the shredded cabbage, some cilantro leaves, and a few slices of tomato. Roll the tacos up snugly and secure each with 3 small picks at even intervals (be sure the picks are catching both layers of tortilla). Cut the tortillas between the picks into 3 pieces.

Arrange the taco pieces on a platter and serve.

MAKES 18 MINI TACOS

▲ Double all the ingredients, cooking the fish in batches.
▼ Halve all the ingredients.
☺ Best cooked and assembled shortly before serving, though they hold up well at room temperature for a couple of hours.

Shrimp Cakes in Shiso Leaves

Shiso is a really wonderful, if not common, herb that's been popping up in more recipes lately. A member of the mint family, it has flavor reminiscent of mint but more complex, with hints of basil and sweet grass. I'm so enamored of this herb I now have a few plants of it in my garden. If you're unable to find shiso (look in specialty produce sections or at Asian markets), you can use strips of red leaf lettuce instead. Keep the greens wrapped in damp paper towels until just before serving, to keep them fresh and crisp.

1 pound medium shrimp, peeled and deveined

¼ cup finely chopped onion or shallot

3 tablespoons finely chopped fresh cilantro

2 tablespoons freshly squeezed lime juice

1 teaspoon Asian fish sauce or soy sauce

¼ teaspoon finely grated lime zest

Dash Sriracha or other hot pepper sauce, plus more to taste

1 egg, lightly beaten

2 to 3 tablespoons olive oil

¼ cup dried bread crumbs

10 large shiso leaves, halved lengthwise, or 20 small shiso leaves

Finely chop the shrimp by hand or in the food processor. If you are using the food processor, pulse just 5 or 6 shrimp at a time until finely chopped, to avoid turning them into a paste. Put the chopped shrimp in a bowl and stir in the onion, cilantro, lime juice, fish sauce, lime zest, and Sriracha. Add the beaten egg and stir until well blended. Cover and refrigerate for 30 minutes to firm up before cooking.

Preheat the oven to 250°F.

Heat 2 tablespoons of the olive oil in a large skillet, preferably nonstick, over medium heat. Stir the bread crumbs into the shrimp mixture, making sure it's thoroughly blended. Spoon the shrimp mixture by the tablespoon into the skillet, forming each into a slightly oval cake about 1¼ inches wide. Cook until lightly browned on the bottom, 2 to 3 minutes, then turn and continue cooking until browned on the other side and opaque through, 2 to 3 minutes longer. Transfer the cakes to a heatproof plate and keep warm in the oven while cooking the rest; add more olive oil to the skillet as needed. You should have about 20 shrimp cakes.

To serve, lay the shiso leaves, overlapping, to one side of a serving plate or platter. Arrange the shrimp cakes on the rest of the platter. Encourage your guests to use one of the shiso leaves to pick up a shrimp cake, wrapping the leaf around the cake to eat it.

MAKES ABOUT 20 CAKES

▲ Double or triple all the ingredients.

▼ Halve all the ingredients.

☺ Prepare the shrimp mixture up to 2 hours ahead, cover, and refrigerate. Fry the cakes up to 3 hours ahead, refrigerate when cooled, and reheat in 250°F oven before serving.

Roasted Red Potatoes with Bacon-Chive Crème Fraîche

Choose baby red potatoes of roughly the same size, so portions and cooking time will be relatively even. To add another layer of flavor to the topping, you can stir in ¼ cup of crumbled blue cheese as well. The topping will be thick enough to perch neatly on top of the potato halves, a one-bite wonder that packs baked-potato-with-the-works flavor.

15 baby red potatoes (about 1 pound), scrubbed

2 tablespoons olive oil

Salt and freshly ground black pepper

4 ounces thick-cut bacon

½ cup crème fraîche

¼ cup finely chopped fresh chives

Preheat the oven to 400°F.

Halve the potatoes and put them in a large bowl. Drizzle the olive oil over, add a good pinch of salt, and toss well to evenly coat. Arrange the potatoes, cut side up, in a roasting pan. For potatoes that don't sit evenly on their own, cut a thin slice from the rounded bottom to make them more stable. Roast until tender and lightly browned, 25 to 30 minutes. Set aside to cool.

While the potatoes are roasting, fry the bacon in a skillet over medium-high heat until browned and crisp. Drain on a paper towel–lined plate, then finely chop or crumble the bacon.

Stir together the crème fraîche, bacon, and 3 tablespoons of the chives in a small bowl. Season to taste with salt and pepper.

To serve, arrange the potatoes on a platter, top each with a dollop of the crème fraîche mixture, sprinkle the remaining chives over, and serve.

MAKES 30 POTATO HALVES

▲ Double or triple all the ingredients.

▼ Halve all the ingredients.

☺ Make the topping up to 1 day ahead, cover, and refrigerate. Let the topping come to room temperature before serving. The potatoes are best roasted shortly before serving.

Meringues with Fresh Berry Filling

These little meringues are wonderfully versatile edible dessert containers. Sweetening berries always brings out their flavorful juices. Some of the juice is used in the whipped cream filling, but too much would make the filling too soft. Save the remaining juice to spoon over ice cream or add to a glass of lemonade.

2 egg whites

Pinch salt

$1/2$ cup plus 2 tablespoons sugar

1 cup finely chopped fresh berries (blackberries, raspberries, and/or strawberries)

$1/3$ cup whipping cream

Small berries or berry pieces, for garnish

Preheat the oven to 225°F. Line a baking sheet with a silicone baking mat or with parchment paper.

Whip the egg whites in an electric mixer at medium speed until quite frothy. Add the salt, increase the speed to medium-high, and begin gradually adding $1/2$ cup of the sugar. Continue beating until the $1/2$ cup of the sugar has been added and the egg whites are glossy and firm, about 5 minutes total.

Use 2 small spoons to form 24 dollops of meringue on the baking sheet. Use the back of one spoon to form each dollop into a 2-inch circle, and leave an indentation in the center of each meringue.

Bake the meringues until firm, about 1 hour, rotating the tray halfway through for even cooking. Take the tray from the oven and let cool fully before removing the meringues. Store them in an airtight container until you are ready to serve.

Put the berries in a bowl and sprinkle with the remaining 2 tablespoons of the sugar. Set aside for 30 minutes, stirring occasionally.

Whip the cream until stiff peaks form, drizzling in about 1 tablespoon of the berry juice toward the end. Use a slotted spoon to lift the berries from the bowl, waiting a few moments for excess juice to drip away, and add the berries to the whipping cream. Fold the berries into the cream and refrigerate until you are ready to serve.

Fill each meringue with a spoonful of the berry cream. Top with a fresh berry and arrange on a platter to serve.

MAKES 24 MERINGUES

▲ Double all the ingredients, baking the meringues on 2 trays and switching them halfway through.

▼ Hard to halve the meringue mixture. You can halve the filling and fill half the meringues, saving extra meringues for a day or two.

☺ Make meringues up to 3 days ahead and store in an airtight container, though humid weather seriously affects their crispness. Make the berry mixture up to 2 hours ahead, cover, and refrigerate; assemble just before serving.

Orange Tuile Cones with Cassata Filling

Silicone baking mats are most valuable with these thin cookies, which can be fiddly, assuring they don't stick to the pan. Once you have the mats in your kitchen you'll use them for countless other baking needs.

To form the cones, a pizzelle roller is an ideal tool. Otherwise, it's easy to make a cone form with a 4-inch-square piece of thin cardboard secured with tape. Cover the cone with aluminum foil before using. It's important to be sure the candied orange peel is evenly and finely chopped for the filling, to avoid blocking the piping bag when filling the cones.

ORANGE TUILES

¾ cup all-purpose flour

¾ cup powdered sugar

2 egg whites

¼ cup unsalted butter, melted and cooled

3 tablespoons freshly squeezed orange juice

¼ teaspoon finely grated orange zest

CASSATA FILLING

½ cup whipping cream

½ cup powdered sugar

1 teaspoon pure vanilla extract

1 cup whole-milk ricotta cheese

⅓ cup coarsely grated semisweet chocolate

⅓ cup finely chopped candied orange peel

Preheat the oven to 400°F. Line 2 baking sheets with silicone baking mats.

To make the tuiles, sift together the flour and sugar into a small bowl. Beat the egg whites with a whisk in a medium bowl until lightly frothy. Gradually add the flour-sugar mixture and whisk until smooth. Add the melted butter, orange juice, and orange zest and whisk gently until evenly blended.

Spoon 6 dollops (1 generous teaspoon each) onto one of the baking sheets, about 4 inches apart. Use the back of the spoon to spread each into an even circle about 3 inches across. Bake until the cookies are lightly browned around the edges, about 5 minutes. While still warm, lift one of the rounds from the baking sheet with a thin spatula and wrap it around the cone form (see headnote). Hold for a few seconds until set, then set aside on a wire rack to cool. Repeat with the remaining rounds; as they become too cool to roll without cracking, put the tray back in the oven for a minute before continuing. Repeat with the remaining batter, alternating baking sheets to start with a cool sheet for each batch. You should have about 30 cones.

To make the filling, whip the cream (with a mixer or by hand) until soft peaks form, then add the powdered sugar and vanilla and continue whipping until medium peaks form. Put the ricotta in a bowl and stir to soften a bit. Stir in the chocolate and orange peel. Gently fold in the whipped cream until well blended. Cover and refrigerate for at least 2 hours before using.

To assemble, spoon the ricotta mixture into a pastry bag fitted with a 3/8-inch plain tip, or into a heavy-duty resealable plastic bag. If you are using the plastic bag, cut off 3/8 inch from one bottom corner. Pipe the filling into the tuile cones, arrange on a platter, and serve.

MAKES ABOUT 30 CONES

▲ Double all the ingredients, but assembly is time-consuming.

▼ Halve all the ingredients.

☺ Make the tuile cones up to 2 days ahead and store in an airtight container. Make the filling to up 1 day ahead, cover, and refrigerate. Assemble the cones shortly before serving.

GASTRO GAMES: FOOD LOVER'S TRIVIA
(We3Chefs.com, 2005)

This game is an interesting twist on the more common "answer question, get game token" format of most trivia games. Players start with one chip from each category: beverages, geography and culture, ingredients, recipes, food people. The categories are color-coded and the chips food themed, so your red chip might have a lobster on it, your orange one a wedge of cantaloupe, green a bunch of asparagus. Then as you answer questions based on a roll of the colored die, you take away a chip with each correct response. So the first clean plate—the player with all the food chips removed—is the winner. There is the occasional piece-of-cake question in the mix, particularly the multiple choicers, but there are quite a lot of stumpers in there, too.

Mocha Cheesecake Bars

The ever-popular cheesecake makes an easy transition to game night, taking on a shallower square form that's easy to cut into finger-friendly pieces. If you're unable to find simple chocolate wafer cookies (the Nabisco brand wafers are a great choice), use graham cracker crumbs for the crust instead.

1¼ cups very fine chocolate wafer cookie crumbs (4 to 5 ounces of cookies)

¼ cup unsalted butter, melted

3 ounces semisweet chocolate, chopped

2 tablespoons Kahlua or other coffee liqueur

1 tablespoon instant espresso powder

12 ounces cream cheese, at room temperature

¾ cup sugar

2 eggs

Preheat the oven to 350°F.

Combine the cookie crumbs and melted butter in a bowl and stir to evenly mix. Put the crumb mixture in a 9-inch square baking pan and press the crumbs evenly across the bottom. Bake the crust until set, about 10 minutes. Set aside to cool. Reduce the oven temperature to 325°F.

Melt the chocolate in the top of a double boiler over medium heat, stirring occasionally. Remove the chocolate from the heat and stir in the coffee liqueur and espresso powder. Set aside to cool.

Combine the cream cheese and sugar in the bowl of a stand mixer fitted with the paddle attachment and whip at medium speed until well blended. Add the eggs and continue beating to make a smooth batter, scraping down the sides of the bowl as needed. Use a rubber spatula to fold in the chocolate mixture until thoroughly incorporated.

Pour the batter onto the cooled crust and spread it out evenly. Bake the cheesecake until set, 35 to 40 minutes. Set aside on a wire rack to cool completely, then refrigerate for at least 2 hours before serving.

Cut the cheesecake into 5 strips each direction, for 25 squares. Arrange them on a platter or tray and serve.

MAKES 25 CHEESECAKE BARS

▲ Double all the ingredients, making the cheesecake in 2 pans.
▼ Best not to halve; extra will keep well for a few days, covered and refrigerated.
☺ Make the cheesecake up to 2 days ahead, cover, and refrigerate.

Cinnamon Meringues with Chocolate Mousse

This is just one aromatic and rich example of how versatile meringues can be. It is a great option for capping off a night of other robust, spicy flavors, such as Curried Coconut Soup with Shrimp (page 121) or Mole Flank Steak with Pickled Peppers (page 52).

MERINGUES

1/2 cup granulated sugar

1 1/2 teaspoons ground cinnamon

2 egg whites

Pinch salt

CHOCOLATE MOUSSE

6 ounces semisweet chocolate, chopped

1/2 cup crème fraîche

1/2 cup whipping cream

1/4 cup powdered sugar

Preheat the oven to 225°F. Line a baking sheet with a silicone baking mat or with parchment paper.

To make the meringues, stir together the granulated sugar and cinnamon in a small dish. Whip the egg whites in an electric mixer at medium speed until quite frothy. Add the salt, increase the speed to medium-high, and gradually add the cinnamon-sugar. Continue beating until all the sugar has been added and the egg whites are glossy and firm, about 5 minutes total.

Use 2 small spoons to form 24 dollops of meringue on the baking sheet. Use the back of one spoon to form each dollop into a 2-inch circle, and leave an indentation in the center of each meringue.

Bake the meringues until firm, about 1 hour, rotating the tray about halfway through for even cooking. Take the tray from the oven and let cool fully before removing the meringues. Store them in an airtight container until you are ready to serve.

To make the chocolate mousse, melt the chocolate in the top of a double boiler over medium heat, stirring occasionally. Set aside to cool to room temperature.

When the chocolate is cool, whip the crème fraîche and cream to stiff peaks, adding the powdered sugar about halfway through. Gently fold the whipped cream mixture into the cooled chocolate. Fill each meringue with a generous dollop of the chocolate mousse and arrange on a platter or tray to serve.

MAKES 24 MERINGUES

▲ Double all the ingredients, baking the meringues on 2 trays and switching them halfway through.

▼ Hard to halve. You can assemble fewer meringues, saving extra mousse and meringues for a day or two.

☺ Make the meringues up to 3 days ahead and store in airtight container, though humid weather seriously affects their crispness. Make the chocolate mousse up to 1 day ahead and refrigerate. Assemble just before serving.

4 SANDWICHES

How could I let pass an opportunity to tip my hat to John Montagu, the Fourth Earl of Sandwich? He may or may not have been the first person to put a piece of meat between two slices of bread to sustain him while gambling, but he is nonetheless namesake to one of the most inescapable culinary compositions of all time. Dandy game-friendly fare it is, a category that has wide-ranging options for game night, from beloved chicken salad to an oddball interpretation of peanut butter and jelly.

Petits Croque Monsieurs

A true sitting-at-a-café-in-Paris croque monsieur has delicious melty cheesiness on the outside as well as inside, a fork-and-knife consideration. I've taken the cheese completely inside, to make this a tasty but tidy game-friendly sandwich. And I've added tomato, which I think always makes grilled cheese more outstanding.

24 slices white cocktail bread

¼ cup unsalted butter, at room temperature

1 cup finely grated Gruyère, Cantal, or Comté cheese

12 thin slices plum tomato

4 ounces thinly sliced Black Forest ham, cut into 2-inch strips

2 tablespoons Dijon mustard

Preheat the oven to 450°F.

Lay 12 of the bread slices on the counter and spread them with half of the butter. Arrange the cheese as neatly and evenly as you can on the butter, then top with the tomato slices. Add the strips of ham, folding them over to fit neatly on the bread. Spread the mustard on the remaining 12 slices of bread and top the sandwiches with them, mustard down. Spread the remaining butter on the tops of the sandwiches.

Arrange the sandwiches on a rimmed baking sheet and set another baking sheet directly on top, to press lightly on the sandwiches and keep the tops from drying out. Bake until the cheese has melted, 8 to 10 minutes. Remove the top baking sheet and turn on the broiler to lightly brown the tops, 1 to 2 minutes.

Transfer the sandwiches to a platter and serve; set on a warming tray to keep warm, if you wish.

MAKES 12 SANDWICHES

▲ Double all the ingredients.

▼ Halve all the ingredients.

⊘ Assemble the sandwiches up to 1 hour before baking, cover with plastic wrap, and refrigerate. Bake shortly before serving.

Chicken Salad Sandwiches with Orange and Walnuts

Leftover cooked chicken is ideal for this recipe, if you have any on hand; you'll need about 1½ cups of it, finely chopped. You have lots of presentation options here, which include serving the chicken salad open-faced on baguette slices, between slices of cocktail bread, or in endive leaves (as for the Salmon Poke on page 60). Just the thing for an evening of chicken foot dominoes!

POACHED CHICKEN BREAST

1 carrot, chopped

1 large celery stalk, chopped

½ cup chopped onion

4 sprigs fresh thyme

1 bay leaf, preferably fresh

½ teaspoon whole peppercorns

1 (10-ounce) boneless skinless
chicken breast

⅔ cup top-quality mayonnaise

½ cup finely chopped toasted
walnuts (see page 9)

⅓ cup finely diced tender
celery stalks

3 tablespoons chopped fresh
flat-leaf parsley

2 tablespoons freshly squeezed
orange juice

1 tablespoon chopped celery leaves

1 teaspoon finely grated orange zest

Salt and freshly ground black pepper

10 slices sandwich bread (whole
wheat or multigrain works well)

For the poached chicken breast, half-fill a saucepan with water and add the carrot, celery, onion, thyme, bay leaf, and peppercorns. Bring the water to a boil over high heat, then reduce the heat to medium and simmer for 10 minutes. Add the chicken breast and simmer until it is no longer pink in the center of the thickest part, 15 to 20 minutes. The chicken should be fully submerged in the water; add more hot water if needed.

Transfer the chicken breast to a paper towel–lined plate and set aside to cool (the cooking liquids can be strained and saved for another use). When cool, finely dice the chicken. In a bowl, combine the chicken, mayonnaise, walnuts, celery, parsley, orange juice, celery leaves, and orange zest. Stir well to mix, then season to taste with salt and pepper.

To serve, spread the chicken salad evenly on 5 of the bread slices and top with the remaining bread. Cut each sandwich into thirds, arrange on a platter, and serve.

MAKES 15 SANDWICHES

▲ Cut the sandwiches into smaller pieces or double all the ingredients.

▼ Halve, using ¾ cup finely chopped cooked chicken.

☺ Make the salad up to 6 hours ahead and refrigerate. Assemble the sandwiches and cut up to 1 hour ahead, cover with plastic wrap, and refrigerate.

Itty Bitty BLTs

Given the widespread popularity that bacon is enjoying, I'm surprised that there isn't yet a bacon-themed board game. (And the Six Degrees of Kevin Bacon game doesn't count.) I'm sure one will be hitting game store shelves near you before long. Probably with scratch-and-sniff, if the game developers know their audience.

This is the time to splurge on the best bacon you can get your hands on, thick slices from a top-of-the-line producer. It may mean a trip to a specialty butcher, or even an order from an online source, such as Neuskes.com. You may find the cocktail-sized loaves in other bread types as well, such as sourdough and rye. Feel free to swap one of those for the pumpernickel, if you wish.

¾ pound top-quality thick-cut bacon

5 to 6 leaves romaine lettuce, tough stems removed

¼ cup top-quality mayonnaise

2 teaspoons finely chopped chives

24 slices pumpernickel cocktail bread, lightly toasted

2 to 3 plum tomatoes, cut into ¼-inch slices

Preheat the oven to 400°F.

Lay the bacon strips on a rimmed baking sheet (it's okay if they touch or even overlap a bit; they'll shrink while cooking). Bake until browned and crisp, 10 to 12 minutes, turning the pieces once or twice. Transfer the bacon to a paper towel–lined plate and let cool. Cut the bacon into 2-inch pieces.

Cut the romaine leaves into lengthwise strips about 2 inches wide. Stir together the mayonnaise and chives in a small bowl.

Spread the mayonnaise onto 12 of the bread slices. Top with a slice or two of the tomato and 2 or 3 pieces of bacon, overlapping. Fold the lettuce strips into 2-inch squares and top the bacon with them. Add the remaining pieces of pumpernickel bread and secure with a frilly toothpick or other small pick. Arrange the sandwiches on a platter or tray for serving.

MAKES 12 SANDWICHES

▲ Double all the ingredients.

▼ Halve all the ingredients.

☺ Prepare individual ingredients up to 4 hours ahead; wrap the bacon well and refrigerate, store the mayonnaise mixture and tomatoes in the refrigerator, wrap the lettuce in damp paper towels and refrigerate, store the bread in an airtight container. Assemble the sandwiches not more than 1 hour before serving and store, covered, in the refrigerator.

Pimento Cheese Tower Sandwiches

It's no Jenga tower of cheese (no, don't even think about it!). This tower instead is constructed of layers of delectable old-school pimento cheese between sheets of tender lavash bread. You can use large (10-inch) flour tortillas instead, though the individual serving pieces won't be as consistent in shape. The cheese mixture also can be simply spread on baguette slices or crackers.

I love Mama Lil's pickled peppers, a delicious product made in my Northwest backyard, but you can use other pickled peppers in their place. Pickled peppers blended with the classic roasted pimentos ramp up the flavor without skewing too far from the original.

8 ounces sharp cheddar cheese, grated (about 3 cups)

1 cup top-quality mayonnaise

1/2 cup finely chopped pimentos, about 1 (4-ounce) jar

1/4 cup finely chopped hot pickled peppers

5 pieces soft lavash bread (9 by 6 inches each)

Combine the cheese and mayonnaise in a food processor and pulse a few times to blend and finely chop the cheese. The mixture should still have some chunky texture.

Transfer the cheese mixture to a medium bowl and fold in the pimentos and peppers until thoroughly blended.

Set one piece of the lavash on a small tray or large plate and spread it evenly with one-quarter of the cheese mixture. Lay a second piece of lavash on top. Repeat the layers three times, topping the tower with the fifth piece of lavash. Gently press down on the bread to compact the layers a bit. Cover with plastic and refrigerate the layered sandwich for at least 1 hour.

Use a serrated knife to cut the sandwich into quarters in each direction, making 16 smaller sandwiches. (For flour tortillas, cut into fifths both vertically and horizontally, for 20 smaller pieces.) Secure each square with a small pick, if you like. Arrange the cheese towers on a platter or tray and serve.

MAKES 16 TO 25 SANDWICHES

▲ Double all the ingredients, making 2 layered sandwiches to cut.

▼ Halve all the ingredients, using 4 1/2 by 6-inch lavash or small flour tortillas.

☺ Layer the sandwich up to 4 hours ahead, cover, and refrigerate. Cut and arrange on a platter up to 1 hour ahead and cover with plastic to keep from drying out.

Pork Tenderloin with Rhubarb Chutney

For this meat-lover's mini open-faced sandwich, roasted pork tenderloin is topped with a vibrant, flavorful rhubarb chutney. When fresh rhubarb isn't available, check the freezer section for frozen. In the fall, consider using fresh cranberries instead, about 2 cups. You may then want to increase the sugar a bit.

1 pork tenderloin (about 1¼ pounds)

1 tablespoon olive oil

1 teaspoon fennel seeds, crushed or ground

Salt and freshly ground black pepper

20 to 24 baguette slices

RHUBARB CHUTNEY

1 tablespoon olive oil

¼ cup finely chopped red onion

½ pound rhubarb, trimmed and sliced

¼ cup firmly packed light brown sugar

2 tablespoons red wine vinegar

Salt

½ teaspoon crushed pink peppercorns, plus more for garnish

Rub the pork tenderloin with the oil, then season it evenly with the fennel seeds and a good pinch each of salt and pepper. Wrap the pork in plastic and refrigerate for at least 30 minutes before cooking.

To make the rhubarb chutney, heat the olive oil in a medium skillet over medium heat. Add the onion and cook, stirring, until tender and lightly browned, 2 to 3 minutes. Add the rhubarb and sauté until beginning to soften, about 3 minutes. Add the brown sugar, vinegar, and a good pinch of salt. Cook, stirring occasionally, until the rhubarb is tender and the chutney is thickened and jamlike, 10 to 15 minutes. Stir in the crushed pink peppercorns. Avoid overstirring the chutney, so some of the rhubarb pieces hold their shape. Set the chutney aside.

Preheat the oven to 400°F. Lay the tenderloin in a baking dish and roast until just barely pink at the thickest part, 20 to 25 minutes (an instant read thermometer should read 145°F). Set aside to cool.

To serve, cut the pork tenderloin into ¼-inch slices and set each on a baguette slice. Top with a dollop of the rhubarb chutney, garnish with a pink peppercorn or two, and serve at room temperature.

MAKES 20 TO 24 OPEN-FACE SANDWICHES

▲ Double or triple all the ingredients.

▼ Hard to halve. Slice fewer portions of pork, refrigerating the rest for a day or two; refrigerate extra chutney.

☺ Make the chutney up to 3 days ahead, cover, and refrigerate (let come to room temperature before serving). Season the pork up to 4 hours ahead; bake not more than 1 hour before serving.

Lamb Burgers with Feta

These tiny burgers with a twist are hearty enough to keep even the most energetic player going. You may need to check ahead with your local meat counter to order ground lamb if they don't carry it regularly. You can easily replace the lamb with ground beef and substitute cheddar or Swiss cheese for the feta, if you like. Thanks to the popularity of mini burgers in recent years, it's getting easier to find mini hamburger buns, though you may need to visit an upscale grocer to find them. In a pinch, you can use slices of baguette, shaping the burgers to match.

2 ounces feta cheese

1½ pounds ground lamb

2 tablespoons minced fresh chives

2 tablespoons minced fresh flat-leaf parsley

1 tablespoon minced or pressed garlic

Salt and freshly ground black pepper

12 mini hamburger buns

12 thin slices plum tomato

12 thin slices cucumber

Cut the feta into relatively even pieces about 1 inch square and ¼ inch thick. (A bit bigger than a Scrabble tile.)

Combine the lamb, chives, parsley, garlic, and a good pinch each of salt and pepper in a bowl. Mix with your hands until thoroughly blended. Separate the lamb mixture into 12 even portions and form each into a 2-inch patty with a piece of the feta in the center.

Preheat an outdoor grill or the broiler. Grill or broil the lamb burgers until just a touch of pink remains at the center, about 8 minutes, turning once. Lightly toast the buns, if you wish.

To serve, set the lamb burgers on the bottom buns, top each with a slice of tomato and cucumber, and add the bun tops. Arrange on a platter and set on a warming tray to keep warm, if you wish.

MAKES 12 BURGERS

▲ Double or triple all ingredients.

▼ Halve all the ingredients.

☺ Form the burgers up to 4 hours ahead, cover, and refrigerate. Grill or broil and assemble just before serving.

Walnut Sablés with Maple-Walnut Cream

These sablé cookies are delicious served as is, if you prefer. But the filling with maple syrup and toasted walnuts adds wonderful flavor and decadence. This is an ideal do-ahead recipe; in fact, the cookies are best not served immediately. Make them at least an hour before serving; they'll still be delicious a day or two later.

WALNUT SABLÉS

1 1/2 cups all-purpose flour

1/3 cup chopped toasted walnuts (see page 9)

1/2 cup powdered sugar

1/2 teaspoon salt

1/2 cup unsalted butter, cut into pieces and chilled

3 egg yolks

1 teaspoon pure vanilla extract

MAPLE WALNUT CREAM

1/2 cup unsalted butter, at room temperature

1 1/2 cups powdered sugar

3 tablespoons pure maple syrup

1/3 cup very finely chopped toasted walnuts (see page 9)

To make the walnut sablés, combine 1/2 cup of the flour and the walnuts in a food processor and pulse until the walnuts are very finely chopped. Add the remaining 1 cup flour, powdered sugar, and salt and pulse a few times to blend. Add the butter and pulse until the mixture has a sandy texture. Add the egg yolks and vanilla and pulse until well blended. Turn the dough out onto a work surface and form it into a disk. Wrap in plastic and refrigerate for at least 30 minutes.

Preheat the oven to 375°F. Line 2 baking sheets with silicone baking mats or parchment paper. Set 2 oven racks at the center-most levels.

To make the maple walnut cream, stir the butter in a bowl to soften and stir in the powdered sugar 1/2 cup at a time, until smooth. Add the maple syrup and walnuts and stir to blend evenly.

Roll out the sablé dough on a lightly floured surface to about 1/4 inch thick (let the dough sit for 10 to 15 minutes if it is too firm to roll right away). Cut the dough into 2-inch rounds and arrange them about 1 inch apart on the baking sheets. If needed, gently re-form the dough trim into a disk and roll out once again to cut enough rounds to make 48 in total.

Bake until firm and lightly browned, 10 to 14 minutes, switching the trays about halfway through for even cooking. Transfer the cookies to a wire rack to cool.

When the cookies are cool, gently spread the bottoms of half the cookies with the maple walnut filling and top with the remaining cookies. You can run your finger around the edge of the filling to tidy it, if you wish. Arrange the cookies on a plate or platter at least 1 hour before serving.

MAKES 24 SANDWICHES

▲ Double all the ingredients, but make the dough in batches.

▼ Hard to halve.

⊘ Make the filling up to 1 day ahead, cover, and refrigerate. Let it come to room temperature before using. Bake the cookies up to 1 day ahead and store in an airtight container. The sandwiches can be made up to 2 days ahead and stored in an airtight container.

PB&J Blondie Bites

Battleship been sunk? The Operation not go so well? Your Cranium just plain Scrabbled out? If you need a little game-night comforting, nothing says "comfort" quite like peanut butter and jelly. This is a tribute to that classic partnership, done up in an unusual dessert fashion. The freezing step makes much easier work of cutting tidy portions of the brownie sandwich, but also lets you hold the dessert for a couple of days before serving.

1 cup natural chunky peanut butter, at room temperature

1/2 cup unsalted butter, at room temperature

1/2 cup firmly packed light brown sugar

2 eggs

1 teaspoon pure vanilla extract

1/2 cup all-purpose flour

1 (8-ounce) container mascarpone

3/4 cup top-quality blackberry, strawberry, or raspberry jam, preferably seedless

Preheat the oven to 350°F. Lightly butter a 9-inch baking pan.

Combine the peanut butter, butter, and brown sugar in the bowl of a stand mixer fitted with a paddle attachment and cream together at medium speed until smooth. Add the eggs, one at a time, blending until smooth. Add the vanilla, scraping down the sides as needed. With the mixer at low speed, add the flour and beat until well blended. Spoon the batter into the baking pan, smoothing the top.

Bake until firm around the edges and a toothpick inserted in the center comes out clean, 30 to 35 minutes. Set aside on a wire rack to cool.

Combine the mascarpone and jam in the bowl of a stand mixer fitted with a whip attachment and whip together at medium-high speed until firm and fluffy, like thick whipped cream, 1 to 2 minutes. Refrigerate until you are ready to use it.

When the blondie is fully cooled, turn it out onto a cutting board. Use a serrated knife to cut it in half horizontally. Return the bottom portion to the baking pan cut side up. (Use a piece of clean cardboard to slip under the portion to help move it more easily.) Spread the mascarpone mixture evenly over and top with the other half of the blondie, cut side down. Cover the pan with foil and freeze until the mascarpone is solid, 2 hours or more.

At least 30 minutes before serving, run a small knife around the edge of the frozen blondie and turn it out onto a cutting board. Use a large chef's knife to cut the blondies (still frozen) into 25 squares and transfer them to a serving plate or platter to serve. As the mascarpone thaws it will become soft and creamy again.

MAKES 25 SANDWICHES

▲ Double all the ingredients, baking the brownies in 2 pans.

▼ Best not to halve; extra will keep well for a day, covered and refrigerated.

☉ Layer the brownie and freeze up to 5 days before serving; unmold and cut the brownies up to 2 hours before serving.

GASTRO GAMES: A FEW FOR THE KIDS (IN ALL OF US)

SLAMWICH (Gamewright, 1994) I have the snazzy "collector's edition" of this game, which comes in a mini tin lunch box! Kids ages 6 and up can play, and they may have an advantage over us grown-ups with slower reflexes and dwindling eyesight. Cards—most of which are sandwich ingredients, from bologna to gummy worms—are flipped onto a central pile and you gain strides by slamming your hand on the pile when certain cards or combinations pop up. Just watch out for the sandwich thieves (a dog, some pretty strong ants) and the munchers!

ALFREDO'S FOOD FIGHT (Fundex Games, 2005) This may not be the right kind of message for young foodies out there, but a fake food fight is surely better than a real one. A chef figure twirls in the center of the table while players use cool little flinging forks to propel their meatballs (with spaghetti yarn attached) at the poor guy. The first to get all their meatballs to stick wins.

GREEN EGGS AND HAM SPEEDY DINER GAME (I Can Do That Games, 2008) The perennial favorite childhood gem of the inimitable Dr. Seuss comes to board-game life. For each round, one player is the chef (complete with a little chef hat to wear), calling out orders while other players race to pick up the food and deliver it to the correct customer. Mayhem ensues. Especially if sugar's been served to the preschoolers.

Ice Cream Sandwiches

Vanilla ice cream may be one of the world's most perfect foods. Not only is the frozen treat delicious in its state of natural simplicity, a carton of vanilla ice cream is pretty much any flavor of ice cream waiting to happen. It's what I use for this array of options for homemade ice cream sandwiches. This recipe is really more a slew of ideas than a specific formula. I have, on a few occasions, gone to the effort of making both the cookies and the ice cream for ice cream sandwiches. But honestly, it takes loads of time and considering the time-to-pleasure ratio, I'm convinced that taking the right shortcuts produces really tasty ice cream sandwiches that will wildly impress your friends.

PICK A COOKIE: It should be sturdy enough to hold the ice cream firmly, without being too hard; stick with smaller cookies (not much more than 2½ inches across) to suit the game-play setting. You should need about 32 cookies, to make 16 sandwiches, though this will vary with the size of cookie used.

- Chocolate chip cookies
- Chocolate wafers
- Gingersnaps
- Oatmeal cookies
- Peanut butter cookies
- Shortbread

PICK A FLAVOR: You can definitely buy mint chocolate chip or caramel ripple ice cream if you prefer, but it's great fun to customize the ice cream filling to match the cookie and your inspirations. Start with 1 quart of a top-quality vanilla ice cream. Note that alcohol impedes freezing; don't go overboard adding spirits, and plan on a little longer freezing time for the blend to become solid again.

- Cognac-soaked raisins or chopped prunes
- Crushed amaretti cookies
- Crushed fresh berries
- Espresso powder mixed with a bit of water
- Finely chopped candied ginger
- Grated bittersweet chocolate
- Mint liqueur
- Peanut butter
- Toasted coconut

PICK A FINISH: Sometimes the simplest techniques add the greatest panache; a flick of the wrist and the edges of your ice cream sandwiches will have a flavor and visual boost from one of these finishing touches. After making the sandwiches, freeze them for at least an hour to set up a bit, then roll the edges and continue freezing. About ¾ cup of your chosen finisher should be enough for your sandwiches.

- Finely chopped chocolate-mint wafers
- Finely chopped toasted nuts (hazelnuts, walnuts, almonds, pecans)
- Finely crushed candies (toffee, peppermints)
- Grated chocolate
- Toasted coconut

CONTINUED

Now comes the fun. Pick an element from each category, items that sound complementary and delicious (or two or three combos, for some variety) and get rolling.

Transfer a carton of top-quality vanilla ice cream from the freezer to the fridge and let it soften until easy to scoop, 30 to 60 minutes.

Scoop the ice cream into a bowl and stir in the flavoring of choice. The amount needed will vary, from just a few tablespoons of intensely flavored espresso to perhaps 1 cup of toasted coconut. Put the bowl in the freezer for 30 to 60 minutes to firm up a bit (longer if alcohol's been used).

Use a small scoop to top your cookies with the ice cream. A spring-loaded scoop will be most efficient. Top with another cookie, pressing down at the center just enough to squeeze the ice cream to the edge of the cookie. Set the sandwich on a baking sheet and put in the freezer while making the remaining sandwiches.

Once the sandwiches have been made, roll the edges in a finishing touch of choice, before the ice cream is fully firm. Freeze on the tray until frozen solid, then transfer the sandwiches to a heavy-duty resealable plastic bag, or just cover the tray well with aluminum foil.

The sandwiches will be best the next day; they can be stored for up to 1 week before serving.

MAKES ABOUT 16 SANDWICHES

Banana Bread with Hazelnut–Cream Cheese Filling

This banana bread recipe melds one of James Beard's variations with a few touches from my mother's recipe. During the holiday season you can use a top-quality fruitcake in place of the banana bread, perhaps adding a small drizzle of rum or brandy to the filling.

BANANA BREAD

$1/2$ cup unsalted butter, at room temperature

$1/2$ cup sugar

$1/4$ cup honey

2 eggs

3 large very ripe bananas, mashed

$1/4$ cup buttermilk

$1 3/4$ cups all-purpose flour

1 teaspoon baking soda

$1/2$ teaspoon salt

$3/4$ cup coarsely chopped toasted hazelnuts (see page 9)

FILLING

8 ounces cream cheese, at room temperature

$1/2$ cup finely chopped toasted hazelnuts (see page 9)

$1/2$ cup powdered sugar

$1/2$ teaspoon ground cinnamon

$1/2$ teaspoon pure vanilla extract

Preheat the oven to 350°F. Generously butter a 9 by 5-inch loaf pan. Cut a strip of parchment to line the length of the pan with a couple inches excess at either end. Butter the paper. (The paper is optional but serves as extra insurance against sticking.)

Combine the butter, sugar, and honey in the bowl of a stand mixer fitted with the paddle attachment and cream at medium speed until light and fluffy. Beat in the eggs, one at a time, then beat in the bananas and buttermilk, scraping down the sides of the bowl as needed. Sift together the flour, baking soda, and salt onto a piece of waxed paper. With the mixer at low speed, slowly add the dry ingredients and nuts and mix just to blend.

Spoon the batter into the loaf pan and smooth the surface. Bake until the bread is nicely browned and a toothpick inserted in the center comes out clean, about 1 hour. Let cool for a few minutes in the pan, then turn the bread out onto a wire rack. Carefully turn it back upright and cool completely.

To make the filling, stir the cream cheese in a bowl with a wooden spoon to soften it. Stir in the hazelnuts, powdered sugar, cinnamon, and vanilla. Let sit at room temperature until the banana bread is cooled completely.

Trim the ends from the bread and cut into 12 slices. Spread 6 slices with the filling and top with the remaining slices. Cut each sandwich into thirds and arrange on a serving tray.

MAKES 18 SANDWICHES

▲ Double all the ingredients, making the bread in 2 batches; or cut sandwiched slices into smaller pieces for more portions.

▼ Hard to reduce, though extra sandwiches will keep for 1 to 2 days, well wrapped and refrigerated.

☺ Make bread and filling up to 2 days ahead; store the bread well wrapped and the filling covered and refrigerated. The assembled sandwich pieces can be held in the refrigerator for up to 3 hours before serving.

5

P A S T R I E S

Pastries both savory and sweet lend themselves well to game play. Dough of all types, from yeasty bread dough to buttery pastry, can create self-contained packets to enclose, cradle, or otherwise support countless delicious fillings and toppings. And a few are plan-ahead jackpots, recipes that can be made well in advance, frozen, and baked just in time for the first roll of the dice.

Almost Bite-Sized Pizzas

Who says pizzas have to be round? But if you did cut some small rounds to go with these squares, you could play an edible game of tic-tac-toe! With three or four easy toppings at hand, you can quickly make up a few different combos for your guests. The tomato sauce recipe makes about twice as much as you need, but it's not practical to make it in smaller batches. You'll be thrilled to have the great sauce on hand, to toss with pasta or sautéed shrimp, or freeze for another batch of pizza! Or shortcut things with a top-quality tomato sauce instead.

TOMATO SAUCE

2 tablespoons olive oil

1/2 cup finely chopped onion

3 cloves garlic, minced or pressed

1 (14 1/2-ounce) can chopped tomatoes, preferably San Marzano

1 tablespoon minced fresh basil, or 1 teaspoon dried

1 teaspoon minced fresh oregano, or 1/2 teaspoon dried

PIZZA DOUGH

2 cups all-purpose flour, plus more as needed

1 teaspoon salt

3/4 cup warm (about 105°F) water

1 teaspoon (1/2 envelope) active dry yeast

2 tablespoons olive oil

TOPPINGS

4 large mushrooms, trimmed and thinly sliced

2 ounces pepperoni, thinly sliced

1/4 cup sliced black olives

2 cups grated mozzarella cheese

1/2 cup thinly sliced red onion

To make the tomato sauce, heat the olive oil in a saucepan over medium heat. Add the onion and garlic and cook, stirring occasionally, until tender and aromatic, 3 to 5 minutes. Add the tomatoes, basil, and oregano and continue cooking until slightly thickened and aromatic, about 20 minutes. Set aside to cool, then purée the sauce with an immersion blender or in a food processor. Refrigerate until it is needed.

To make the dough, combine the flour and salt in a bowl and stir to mix. Make a well in the center, pour the warm water into the well and sprinkle the yeast over. Set aside until the yeast is frothy, about 5 minutes. Stir the dough for a few moments with a wooden spoon, drawing in the flour from the edges, then drizzle the olive oil over. Continue to stir the dough until it begins to come together in a ball. Transfer it to a lightly floured work surface and knead the dough until it becomes smooth and satiny, about 10 minutes, adding a bit more flour if needed. Put the dough in a lightly oiled bowl (it could be the same bowl in which you mixed the dough) and turn it to evenly but lightly coat with oil. Cover the bowl with a clean kitchen towel and set aside in a warm place until the dough has doubled in bulk, about 1 hour.

Preheat the oven to 375°F. Line 2 baking sheets with silicone baking mats or parchment paper. Set 2 oven racks on the centermost levels.

Turn the risen dough out onto a lightly floured work surface and punch it down. Using your palms, press the dough out into a rectangle to get things started, then use a rolling pin to roll the

CONTINUED ▶

dough to a rectangle about 10 inches by 20 inches. The gluten developed in the dough will resist rolling and spring back at times. If this becomes troublesome, let the dough sit to relax for a few minutes, then continue rolling.

Cut the dough, preferably using a rolling-blade pizza cutter, into 2½-inch squares. Transfer the squares to the baking sheets, with about 1 inch between them. Spread a thin smear of tomato sauce over the squares and top with the pepperoni, a mushroom slice or two, and/or olive slices, finishing with a sprinkling of mozzarella and a few pieces of onion.

Bake until the dough is lightly browned and the cheese is melted, 15 to 17 minutes, switching the sheets halfway through for even cooking. Transfer the pizzas to a platter for serving, setting it on a warming tray to keep warm, if you wish.

MAKES 32 MINI PIZZAS

▲ Double all the ingredients.

▼ Use half of the dough; wrap the extra well (after punching it down from the rise) and freeze (up to 1 month) for another use. Save extra tomato sauce for another use. Halve the toppings.

☺ Make the sauce up to 4 days ahead and refrigerate. The pizzas are best freshly baked, but you can bake earlier in the day and gently reheat in a 250°F oven before serving.

Olive and Cheese Crackers

This harkens to a recipe I remember my mom making for virtually every party my folks hosted at our house when I was a kid. Granted, the original recipe called for oleo and "one small glass of sharp cheddar cheese." I'd probably still love that version today, but I have updated it nonetheless; it remains a tribute to the memory of my mother.

¾ cup finely chopped pimento-stuffed olives

2¼ cups all-purpose flour

1 cup unsalted butter, at room temperature

1 cup finely grated sharp cheddar cheese

½ teaspoon salt

¼ teaspoon cayenne pepper

Dry the olives a bit on a paper towel, then toss them with ¼ cup of the flour, working quickly to evenly coat the olives without the flour clumping.

Combine the butter and cheese in the bowl of a stand mixer fitted with the paddle attachment and cream together at medium speed. Working at low speed, blend in the olives, salt, and cayenne. Gradually add the remaining 2 cups flour, working just until it is evenly incorporated and the dough begins to come together.

Transfer the dough to a 20-inch piece of waxed or parchment paper and form the dough into a log about 1¾ inches in diameter. Wrap well and refrigerate for about 1 hour.

Preheat the oven to 400°F. Set 2 oven racks on the centermost levels.

Unwrap the dough and cut it into ⅜-inch slices. Arrange the slices 1 inch apart on 2 ungreased baking sheets. Bake until firm and lightly browned around the edges, about 20 minutes, switching the pans halfway through for even baking. Let cool for a few minutes on the baking sheets, then transfer the crackers to a wire rack to cool completely.

Arrange the crackers on a platter or tray and serve.

MAKES ABOUT 4 DOZEN CRACKERS

▲ Double all the ingredients, making the dough in 2 batches.

▼ Halve all the ingredients. Or slice and bake fewer crackers, freezing the remaining dough for another time.

☺ Make dough up to 1 day ahead and refrigerate. Or make it up to 1 month ahead, wrap well, and freeze. The crackers are best enjoyed the day they are baked, but can be stored in an airtight container for up to 1 day.

Roasted Fennel Focaccia with Pecorino

A delicious snack to enjoy as is, these fingers of focaccia can be served with small dishes of tomato sauce (page 95 or your favorite prepared sauce) alongside, warmed and served in small bowls for dipping. Garlic lovers may want to work in the tender roasted cloves of a small head of garlic, coarsely chopped (see page 9).

Depending on the size and moisture content of your fennel bulb, you may need to add as much as 1/2 cup or more extra flour.

1 medium fennel bulb

3 tablespoons plus 2 teaspoons olive oil

2 1/2 cups all-purpose flour, more if needed

1 1/2 teaspoons salt

1/4 teaspoon freshly ground black pepper

3/4 cup warm (about 105°F) water

2 teaspoons (1 envelope) active dry yeast

1/2 cup freshly grated Pecorino or Parmesan cheese

Preheat the oven to 425°F.

Trim the stalks from the fennel bulb, reserving the tender green fronds. Cut the tough base from the bulb, then halve the bulb vertically. Set the fennel halves on a piece of aluminum foil, drizzle with 2 teaspoons of the olive oil, and wrap up loosely in the foil. Bake until tender, about 1 hour. Set aside to cool.

When the fennel is cool, cut away the core and finely chop the flesh. Chop enough of the reserved fennel fronds to make 1/4 cup.

Put the flour, salt, and pepper in the bowl of a stand mixer fitted with the paddle attachment and stir to mix. Make a well in the center. Pour the warm water into the well and sprinkle the yeast over. Let sit until the yeast is frothy, about 5 minutes.

Mix the wet and dry ingredients at low speed for a few seconds, then drizzle the remaining 3 tablespoons of the olive oil over and sprinkle in the fennel fronds. Continue to mix until the dough begins to come together. Add the roasted fennel and continue mixing until the dough is cohesive, adding more flour if the dough is quite sticky. With the mixer's dough hook or working the dough by hand, knead the dough until it becomes smooth and satiny, and it pulls cleanly away from the sides of the bowl or the work surface, about 10 minutes, adding more flour if needed. Put the dough in a lightly oiled bowl (it could be the same bowl in which you mixed the dough) and turn it to evenly but lightly coat the dough with oil. Cover the bowl with a clean kitchen towel and set aside in a warm place until the dough has doubled in bulk, about 1 hour.

Lightly oil a rimmed baking sheet. Turn the risen dough out onto a lightly floured work surface and punch it down. Using your palms, press the dough out into a rectangle the size of your baking sheet. Carefully transfer the dough to the baking sheet. Cover the pan with the towel and set aside to rise by about half, about 30 minutes.

Preheat the oven to 375°F.

Sprinkle the Pecorino cheese over the dough and bake the focaccia until nicely browned on top, 15 to 18 minutes. Let cool on a wire rack. Transfer the focaccia to a cutting board and cut it in half lengthwise and across into strips about 1½ inches wide. Arrange the pieces on a platter or tray and serve.

MAKES ABOUT 32 PIECES

▲ Double all the ingredients, making the dough in 2 batches.

▼ Hard to halve.

☉ This is best baked not more than 3 hours before serving. Wrap well once fully cooled; you can warm it in a 250°F oven and cut into pieces shortly before serving.

Beef Empanadas with Black Beans and Jalapeño

Many parts of the world have a savory pastry turnover of some kind, from India's samosas to England's pasties, all of which are wonderfully versatile, game-friendly preparations. The empanada touts Spanish roots; the flaky, often meat-filled pastry is common in much of Mexico and South America. You'll find another variation, with a chicken and walnut filling, on page 103.

FILLING

2 tablespoons olive oil

½ cup finely chopped onion

1 tablespoon minced or pressed
    garlic

¾ teaspoon ground cumin

½ pound lean ground beef

⅓ cup canned black beans, drained
    and rinsed

3 tablespoons tomato paste

1 jalapeño chile, cored, seeded,
    and minced

Salt and freshly ground black pepper

DOUGH

2 cups all-purpose flour

1 teaspoon salt

½ cup unsalted butter, cut into
    pieces and chilled

1 egg

1 tablespoon distilled white vinegar

2 tablespoons ice water, plus more
    if needed

To make the filling, heat the olive oil in a skillet over medium heat. Add the onion and garlic and cook, stirring, until tender and aromatic, 2 to 3 minutes. Stir in the cumin and cook for 1 minute longer. Add the ground beef, breaking it into small pieces, and cook until it is no longer pink, 5 to 7 minutes. (If the beef gives off liquid as it cooks, be sure it is fully evaporated before continuing.) Stir in the black beans, tomato paste, and jalapeño until evenly blended. Season the filling to taste with salt and pepper. Set aside to cool.

To make the dough, combine the flour and salt in a food processor and pulse once to blend. Add the butter and pulse until the mixture has a sandy texture. Add the egg and vinegar, then pulse a few times to blend. Drizzle in the water, pulsing a few times as you go. Pinch some of the dough together in your fingers; if it holds its shape and is not crumbly, it's ready. If not, add another couple teaspoons of water and pulse once or twice. Transfer the dough to the work surface and form it into a disk. Wrap in plastic and refrigerate for at least 30 minutes.

Preheat the oven to 400°F. Line a baking sheet with a silicone baking mat or parchment paper.

Cut the dough into 18 equal pieces (each about the size of a walnut). Roll one portion out on a lightly floured work surface to a circle about 4 inches across. If the filling is on the dry side, drizzle a couple teaspoons of water over and stir; the filling should hold its shape but look moist. Top the dough circle with about 1 table-spoon of the filling. Fold in half and press the edges together well, then use your fingers or a fork to crimp the dough edge, securely sealing it. Repeat with the remaining dough and filling.

Set the empanadas on the baking sheet and bake until nicely browned, 15 to 20 minutes. Let cool slightly on the sheet. Transfer the empanadas to a platter for serving, setting the platter on a warming tray to keep warm, if you wish.

MAKES 18 EMPANADAS

▲ Double all the ingredients, making the dough in 2 batches.

▼ Hard to halve. Freeze extra filled empanadas (before baking) for another time.

☺ Make the filling and dough up to 2 days ahead and refrigerate. It is best to bake or freeze shortly after assembling. Freeze filled empanadas on a baking sheet; when solid, transfer to a resealable freezer bag and freeze for up to 1 month. Bake frozen, adding a few minutes to the baking time.

FOR GAME LOVERS: BOARDGAMEGEEK

At www.BoardGameGeek.com you'll find an extensive web-based community for serious board game lovers from around the world. There is plenty on the site to browse as a visitor, or with free registration you can join in forum discussions, rate games, and access deeper aspects of the site. While some BGG members enjoy the occasional game of Wits & Wagers or Taboo, this audience is more devoted to strategy games—which can relate to building civilizations, farming, economics, and history among other themes. Many of these are developed in Europe where game play tends to require good concentration, while in North America many of the games produced tend to provide a chance to unwind. I was a bit humbled to find that of the BGG list of top 100 games as rated by their members, only one is in our game closet: go. But for even a social-casual gamer like myself, BGG offers an astounding resource in its online database of games (which does include most, if not all, of the most popular games out there, even Mouse Trap!) and an engaging, friendly community of gamers to help newbies and veterans alike learn more about the wealth of options in game play available today.

Mushroom and Goat Cheese Tartlets

Working with premade tartlet shells is the ace up your sleeve here. Look for them in specialty food stores and well-stocked groceries, often in the frozen food section. Either regular dough-lined tartlet shells or more delicate phyllo shells can be used. With a flavorful filling that's easy to make, you can turn out delicate tartlets in no time flat.

Crumbled blue cheese can be used in place of the goat cheese, if you prefer. Or offer your guests a choice, making half with each.

2 tablespoons olive oil

8 ounces mushrooms (white button, shiitake, and/or cremini), trimmed and finely chopped

1/4 cup finely chopped onion or shallot

Salt and freshly ground black pepper

2 tablespoons minced fresh flat-leaf parsley

2 eggs

1/2 cup whole milk

24 unsweetened tartlet shells (1 1/2 to 2 inches in diameter)

2 ounces goat cheese, crumbled (about 1/2 cup)

2 tablespoons minced fresh chives

Preheat the oven to 350°F.

Heat the olive oil in a large skillet over medium heat. Add the mushrooms, onion, and a good pinch each of salt and pepper. Cook, stirring often, until the liquid given off by the mushrooms has evaporated, 5 to 7 minutes. Let cool, then stir in the parsley and taste for seasoning, adding more salt or pepper if needed.

Beat the eggs with a fork in a lipped measuring cup, then blend in the milk until smooth.

Spoon about 1 teaspoon of the mushroom mixture into each tartlet shell and set the shells on a rimmed baking sheet. Carefully pour the egg/milk mixture over, filling each shell to just below the edge. Top with a few crumbles of goat cheese and a sprinkle of chives.

Bake the tartlets until the filling is set and the pastry lightly browned, about 25 minutes. Let cool slightly. If the tartlets have foil liners, remove them before transferring the tartlets to a platter. Serve warm (set on a warming tray if you wish) or at room temperature.

MAKES 24 TARTLETS

▲ Double or triple all ingredients, baking the tartlets in batches.
▼ Halve all the ingredients.
☺ Make the mushroom mixture up to 1 day ahead, cover, and refrigerate. The tartlets are best baked not more than 2 hours before serving; refrigerate and gently reheat in a 250°F oven.

Empanadas with Chicken and Walnut

Freestyling is when cooking gets really fun for me. One of my favorite chicken dishes is a sauté with onion, chopped walnuts, and a good dose of paprika. I riff on that combination as a filling for this tender, flaky empanada dough. Feel free to follow your own inspirations for other potential filling candidates.

FILLING

1 carrot, chopped

1 cup coarsely chopped onion

1 clove garlic, crushed

3 sprigs fresh thyme

Salt and freshly ground black pepper

1 small (8-ounce) boneless, skinless chicken breast

1 cup chopped toasted walnuts (see page 9)

1 tablespoon sweet Hungarian paprika

DOUGH

2 cups all-purpose flour

1 teaspoon salt

$1/2$ cup unsalted butter, cut into pieces and chilled

1 egg

1 tablespoon distilled white vinegar

2 tablespoons ice water, more if needed

To make the filling, half-fill a saucepan with water and add the carrot, $3/4$ cup of the onion, garlic, and thyme with a good pinch each of salt and pepper. Bring to a boil over high heat, then reduce the heat to medium and simmer for 10 minutes. Add the chicken breast and simmer until no longer pink in the center of the thickest part, 15 to 20 minutes. The chicken should be fully submerged in the water; add more hot water if needed.

Transfer the chicken breast to a paper towel–lined plate and set aside to cool. Strain the cooking liquids and set aside $3/4$ cup; discard the remaining liquids or save for another use.

When cool, finely dice the chicken and put it in a bowl. Combine the walnuts, remaining $1/4$ cup onion, and paprika in a food processor and pulse a few times. Gradually add $1/2$ cup of the reserved cooking liquids to make a thin paste. Add this to the chicken, with salt and pepper to taste, and stir to evenly blend. The mixture should be moist but still hold its shape; if it seems dry, add a drizzle more of the cooking liquids or water. Refrigerate until it is needed.

To make the dough, combine the flour and salt in a food processor and pulse once to blend. Add the butter and pulse until the mixture has a sandy texture. Add the egg and vinegar, then pulse a few times to blend. Drizzle in the water, pulsing a few times as you go. Pinch some of the dough together in your fingers; if it holds its shape and is not crumbly, it's ready. If not, add another couple of teaspoons of water and pulse once or twice. Transfer the dough to the work surface and form it into a disk. Wrap in plastic and refrigerate for 30 minutes.

Preheat the oven to 400°F. Line a baking sheet with a silicone baking mat or parchment paper.

CONTINUED

Cut the dough into 18 equal pieces (each about the size of a walnut). Roll one portion out on a lightly floured work surface to a circle about 4 inches across. Top the dough circle with about 1 tablespoon of the filling. Fold in half and press the edges together well, then use your fingers or a fork to crimp the dough edge, securely sealing it. Repeat with the remaining dough and filling.

Set the empanadas on the baking sheet. Bake until nicely browned, about 15 minutes. Let cool slightly on the sheet. Transfer the empanadas to a platter for serving and set on a warming tray to keep warm, if you wish.

MAKES 18 EMPANADAS

▲ Double all the ingredients, making the dough in 2 batches.
▼ Hard to halve. Freeze extra filled empanadas (before baking) for another time.
☺ Make the filling and dough up to 2 days ahead; cover the filling, wrap the dough well, and refrigerate. It is best to bake or freeze shortly after assembling. Freeze filled empanadas on a baking sheet; when solid transfer to a resealable freezer bag and freeze for up to 1 month. Bake frozen, adding a few minutes to the baking time.

Chocolate Tartlets with Brandy Cream

I don't condone cheating, but when your friends taste these decadent tartlets, they may be momentarily distracted. From the board. And where their playing pieces are. I'm just saying.

Crisp and delicate phyllo tartlet shells are ideal for this recipe (look for them in the freezer section). You can use other small tartlet shells instead, though depending on their size, you may end up with a couple fewer tartlets. There will be some brandy cream left over, but it would be tough to make a smaller batch. The extra will be delicious as a dip for berries.

BRANDY CREAM

1 egg

¼ cup sugar

2 tablespoons all-purpose flour

¾ cup whipping cream

3 tablespoons brandy

TARTLETS

30 phyllo tartlet shells

5 ounces semisweet chocolate, chopped

2 tablespoons unsalted butter

1 egg

¾ cup whole milk

To make the brandy cream, whisk together the egg, sugar, and flour in a bowl until well blended. Warm ½ cup of the cream in a small saucepan over medium heat until it just comes to a boil. Slowly add the hot cream to the egg mixture, whisking constantly. Return this to the saucepan and cook over medium-low heat, whisking constantly, until thickened, 3 to 4 minutes. Be diligent about whisking continually and evenly across the bottom and edges of the pan to avoid sticking. Take the pan from the heat and whisk in the brandy. Let cool. Whip the remaining ¼ cup of the cream until medium peaks form. Fold this gently into the cooled custard, cover, and refrigerate for at least 1 hour.

Preheat the oven to 350°F. Arrange the tartlet shells on a rimmed baking sheet.

Combine the chopped chocolate and butter in the top of a double boiler and warm over medium heat until melted and smooth, stirring occasionally. Let cool. In a small bowl, beat the egg, then add the milk and whisk gently to mix. Whisk this into the cooled chocolate and transfer to a lipped measuring cup or bowl. Pour the filling into the tartlet shells, filling each not quite to the top. Bake until the filling is puffed and the pastry lightly browned, about 15 minutes. Let cool.

To serve, arrange the tartlets on a platter or serving tray and top each with a dollop of the brandy cream.

MAKES 30 TARTLETS

▲ Double all the ingredients.

▼ Halve all the tartlet ingredients, but not the brandy cream; save extra for another use or use whipped cream instead.

☺ Make the brandy cream up to 1 day ahead and refrigerate. The tartlets can be baked up to 3 hours before serving and left at room temperature.

Nutella and Banana Galettes

This is an example of how a few simple ingredients—sweet pastry, Nutella, and bananas—can conspire to make a wildly delicious treat. The sliced bananas resist browning after a brief dip in fresh orange juice, so they'll remain lovely until your guests' cravings for sweets hit.

SWEET PASTRY DOUGH

1 1/2 cups all-purpose flour

1/3 cup sugar

1/4 teaspoon salt

1/2 cup unsalted butter, cut into pieces and chilled

2 egg yolks

2 tablespoons ice water, plus more if needed

1/2 teaspoon pure vanilla extract

1 large or 2 small ripe (but not soft) bananas

1/2 cup freshly squeezed orange juice

1/2 cup Nutella

2 tablespoons chopped toasted hazelnuts (see page 9)

To make the pastry dough, combine the flour, sugar, and salt in a food processor and pulse to blend. Add the butter and pulse until the mixture has a sandy texture. Add the egg yolks and pulse twice, then add the water and vanilla and pulse a few times to incorporate. Pinch a bit of the dough between your fingers; it should hold its shape without feeling dry. If needed, add another teaspoon or two of water. Turn the dough out onto the work surface and form into a disk. Wrap in plastic and refrigerate for at least 30 minutes.

Preheat the oven to 375°F. Line 2 baking sheets with silicone baking mats or parchment paper. Set 2 oven racks on the center-most levels.

Roll the dough out on a lightly floured surface to a circle about 14 inches across and 1/8 inch thick (let the dough sit for 10 or 15 minutes if it is too firm to roll right away). Use a 2 3/4-inch round cutter (plain or fluted) to cut rounds from the dough. Arrange them about 1 inch apart on the baking sheets. Bake until lightly browned, about 15 minutes, switching the pans about halfway through for even cooking. Let cool slightly on the baking sheets, then transfer the pastry to a wire rack to fully cool.

Cut the banana into 1/4-inch slices and put them in a bowl with the orange juice. Toss gently to be sure that all slices are fully coated in the juice and let sit a few minutes. Transfer the slices to a piece of paper towel and lightly pat the tops to dry. Top each pastry round with 1 teaspoon of the Nutella and spread it out a bit, leaving a 1/2-inch border. Arrange 2 or 3 banana slices, slightly overlapping, on top of the Nutella. Sprinkle the bananas with chopped hazelnuts and arrange on a platter for serving.

MAKES 18 TO 20 GALETTES

▲ Double all the ingredients, making the dough in batches.

▼ Best not to halve. Roll out and use half of the dough, freezing the rest for another time.

☺ Make the dough, wrap well, and refrigerate up to 2 days ahead. Bake and assemble the galettes up to 2 hours before serving.

Raspberry and Cream Cheese Turnovers

Premade puff pastry is one of the key secrets to entertaining with a little panache. Different brands have sheets of different sizes, but many have dimensions that make portioning 3-inch squares easy. If needed, roll out the pastry a bit to get sides measuring 9 or 12 inches. The flavor will be best if you can find puff pastry made with butter, not shortening.

3 ounces cream cheese, at room temperature

1/2 cup powdered sugar

1 pound frozen puff pastry, thawed

3/4 cup fresh whole raspberries (about 3 ounces)

Line 2 baking sheets with silicone baking mats or parchment paper.

Stir the cream cheese in a small bowl until smooth. Add the powdered sugar and stir until evenly blended. Refrigerate while you prepare the dough.

If the dough is soft or your kitchen quite warm, lightly flour the counter to prevent the dough from sticking. Put the dough on the counter and cut into 24 (3-inch) squares (a pizza cutter with its rolling blade is ideal for this).

Stir the raspberries into the cream cheese, breaking them up a bit as you go. Spoon a scant teaspoon of the mixture into the center of each dough square. Dip your finger in a small dish of water and very lightly moisten 2 joining edges of the dough. Fold the opposite corner of the dough over the filling to form a triangle and pinch the edges together with your fingers. Press the pastry edges with the tines of a fork to seal them well. Use the tip of kitchen shears or a small knife to snip a "V" vent in the top center of the dough. Set the turnovers on the baking sheets and refrigerate for 30 to 60 minutes before baking.

Preheat the oven to 400°F. Set 2 oven racks on the centermost levels.

Bake the turnovers until nicely puffed and browned, about 15 minutes, switching the pans halfway through for even baking. Transfer the turnovers to a wire rack to cool. Arrange the pastries on a platter or tray for serving.

MAKES 24 TURNOVERS

▲ Double or triple all the ingredients.

▼ Halve all the ingredients, or freeze extra unbaked turnovers for another time.

☺ Bake or freeze turnovers within an hour of assembly; they are best served the day they are baked. Freeze the turnovers on the baking sheet; when solid, transfer to a resealable freezer bag and freeze for up to 1 month; bake from frozen, adding a few minutes to the baking time.

6 SMALL DISHES

This chapter exemplifies just how adaptable game-night dining can be. Soups and salads can be deliciously downsized, but you'll find snack treats, desserts, even a meat-and-potatoes option as well. With a variety of small dishes, ramekins, shot glasses, and espresso cups on hand, many of your favorite entertaining recipes can be transformed into game-night recipes. Use these as inspiration for your own tiny-dish delights.

Cumin Spiced Nuts

Spiced nuts are a perpetual favorite snack, particularly when served with cocktails. These aromatic, flavorful nuts are great for game-night eats as well. Small cupcake-type paper cups are ideal serving containers here, so guests can nibble the nuts without getting their fingers messy, shaking a few directly into their mouths. I use 2½-inch cups, but you can vary portion sizes easily, serving the nuts in different-sized cups or dishes.

1½ cups large whole shelled nuts
(hazelnuts, blanched almonds,
pecans, cashews)

⅓ cup pine nuts

¼ cup green pumpkin seeds

¼ cup unsalted butter

1 tablespoon ground cumin

1 teaspoon ground coriander

1 teaspoon salt

¼ teaspoon cayenne pepper

Preheat the oven to 350°F.

Combine the nuts and seeds in a bowl. Melt the butter in a small saucepan over medium heat. Add the cumin, coriander, salt, and cayenne and stir to evenly blend.

Drizzle the spice mixture over the nuts, tossing to evenly coat. Scatter the nuts in an even layer on a rimmed baking sheet. Bake until the nuts are lightly browned and aromatic, stirring once or twice, about 20 minutes. Set aside to cool.

Transfer the spiced nuts to small paper cups or other small dishes to serve.

MAKES 20 TO 24 SMALL CUPS

▲ Double or triple all the ingredients.

▼ Halve all the ingredients.

☺ Roast the nuts up to 3 days ahead and store in an airtight container; gently heat in a 250°F oven before serving or serve at room temperature.

Sage Popcorn

Variations on the popcorn theme are many. I've used this technique also with chili powder, adding about $1\frac{1}{2}$ teaspoons to the melted butter before tossing with the popcorn. Try out other herb or spice combinations to suit your fancy.

As noted for the Cumin Spiced Nuts on the facing page, paper cups are the perfect serving dish for this herb-accented popcorn.

3 tablespoons unsalted butter

2 tablespoons minced fresh sage

2 tablespoons olive oil

$\frac{1}{4}$ cup popcorn kernels

Salt

Melt the butter in a small saucepan over medium heat. Stir in the sage and cook until aromatic and vivid green, about 1 minute; set aside.

Heat the oil in a large saucepan over medium heat. Add the popcorn kernels, quickly cover with the lid, and cook, shaking the pan often (and holding the lid on securely), until the popping subsides, 3 to 4 minutes. Take the pan from the heat. (Alternatively, pop the popcorn in an air popper and put in a large bowl.) Drizzle the sage butter over the popcorn, add salt to taste, and shake or toss to evenly coat the popcorn with the butter.

Serve the popcorn in paper cups or other small dishes.

MAKES 20 TO 24 SMALL CUPS

▲ Double all the ingredients; for more, make in separate batches.

▼ Serve in larger dishes for fewer portions.

☺ Best popped and seasoned shortly before serving.

Chilled Avocado Soup with Roasted Poblano Cream

A little taste of the Southwest to get you in the mood for a rowdy game of Texas Hold'em! While you're at it, maybe it's the perfect night for Mini Tostadas with Cumin Black Beans (page 57) and Baby Baja Tacos (page 65) as well.

SOUP

2 small ripe avocados

2 cups vegetable or chicken broth (see box)

⅓ cup thinly sliced green onion, white and pale green portions

¼ cup freshly squeezed lime juice

2 tablespoons tequila

Few dashes Tabasco

Salt

Slivered green onion tops, for garnish (optional)

ROASTED POBLANO CREAM

1 poblano chile

3 tablespoons sour cream

¼ teaspoon ground cumin

Salt

To make the soup, peel, pit, and coarsely chop the avocados. Purée them in a food processor with ½ cup of the broth, the green onion, lime juice, and tequila, scraping down the sides as needed. With the motor running, add the remaining broth. Season to taste with Tabasco and salt. Transfer the soup to a large lipped measuring cup or bowl and refrigerate for at least 2 hours.

To make the roasted poblano cream, roast the chile under the broiler until the skin blackens, turning occasionally to roast evenly, 10 to 15 minutes total. Put the chile in a plastic bag, securely seal it, and set aside to cool. When the chile is cool enough to handle, peel away and discard the skin. Remove the core and seeds and chop the chile.

Put the chopped poblano in the food processor with the sour cream, cumin, and a pinch of salt. Process until very smooth, scraping the sides once or twice. Transfer to a small bowl and refrigerate until you are ready to serve.

To serve, pour the avocado soup into tall shot glasses or espresso cups of about ¼-cup capacity and top each with a small spoonful of the poblano cream. Top the cream with a pinch of green onion slivers and arrange on a tray to serve.

MAKES 14 MINI SOUPS

▲ Double all the ingredients.

▼ Halve all the ingredients, or serve larger portions of the soup in larger glasses.

☺ Make the roasted poblano cream up to 1 day ahead and refrigerate. Make the soup up to 4 hours ahead and refrigerate.

VEGETABLE BROTH

Some commercial varieties of vegetable broth are rather thick and full-flavored, which is great as the base for a pot of vegetable soup, but it can be overpowering in other recipes. Opt for a thinner, lighter broth here. Or consider making your own, which is incredibly easy. Cover chopped carrot, onion, celery, leek, a smashed garlic clove or two, and fresh herbs (flat-leaf parsley, thyme, bay leaves) with water and simmer for about 1 hour, then let cool and strain.

Green Gazpacho

Care for a little game of Red Light Green Light? Although the word "gazpacho" usually brings to mind the red tomato–based recipe, the chilled soup comes in many forms. I love the fresh bright flavor that cucumber brings to this green version, enhanced with green onion, cilantro, and a bit of zip from jalapeño.

. . . .

2 large cucumbers, peeled, seeded, and chopped

1/4 cup plus 1 tablespoon olive oil

3 tablespoons sherry vinegar

1/2 cup water

1/2 cup sliced green onion, white and pale green portions

1/4 cup moderately packed fresh cilantro leaves

1 jalapeño chile, cored, seeded, and chopped

1 clove garlic, crushed

Salt

1/2 cup finely diced white bread (crusts removed)

Combine the cucumbers with 1/4 cup of the olive oil and the vinegar in a blender and process to finely chop, scraping down the sides as needed. Add the water, green onion, cilantro, jalapeño, garlic, and a good pinch of salt and purée until very smooth. Transfer to a bowl and refrigerate for at least 1 hour before serving.

Shortly before serving, heat the remaining 1 tablespoon of the olive oil in a small skillet over medium heat. Add the diced bread and cook, stirring often, until evenly browned and crunchy. Put the croutons in a small serving bowl.

To serve, pour the gazpacho into tall shot glasses or espresso cups of about 1/4-cup capacity and arrange them on a tray. Set the bowl of croutons alongside and have each guest add a sprinkling to their own soup, so they stay crisp.

MAKES 10 TO 12 MINI SOUPS

▲ Double all the ingredients, but make the soup in batches.

▼ Halve all the ingredients or serve in larger portions.

☺ The flavors are best if made not more than 4 hours ahead, but you can make the soup up to 1 day ahead and refrigerate.

Lentil and Carrot Soup with Cilantro Purée

Rich but not at all heavy, this soup features warm, earthy flavors that are capped off by a drizzle of fresh, bright cilantro purée. You'll have more of the purée than needed here (making less would be a bother). Extra will be delicious tossed with steamed vegetables or sautéed shrimp.

CILANTRO PURÉE

1 cup loosely packed fresh cilantro leaves

¼ cup olive oil

SOUP

2 tablespoons olive oil

1 cup finely chopped onion

2 cloves garlic, minced or pressed

1 teaspoon finely grated or minced fresh ginger

1 tablespoon ground coriander

1 cup red lentils

3 cups vegetable or chicken broth, plus more as needed

Salt and freshly ground black pepper

1 cup finely diced carrot

To make the cilantro purée, combine the cilantro and oil in a food processor (a mini processor, if you have one) and process until smooth, scraping down the sides as needed. Transfer to a small bowl and refrigerate until you are ready to serve.

To make the soup, heat the olive oil in a saucepan over medium heat. Add the onion, garlic, and ginger and cook, stirring often, until tender and aromatic, 3 to 4 minutes. Stir in the coriander and cook until well blended and slightly toasty smelling, about 1 minute. Stir in the lentils, followed by the broth. Bring to a boil over medium-high heat, return the heat to medium, and simmer until the lentils are just tender, 10 to 12 minutes. The soup should simmer gently; reduce the heat to medium-low if needed.

Using an immersion blender, whirl the soup for 10 to 15 seconds, to purée about half of the lentils. Or, spoon about 2 cups of the lentils into a blender, purée, and return them to the pan. Season the soup to taste with salt and pepper. Add the carrot and simmer until tender, 5 to 7 minutes. If the soup is quite thick, add ¼ cup or so of broth or water; it should be just thin enough to sip easily from a cup.

To serve, spoon the soup into espresso cups or small glasses of about ½-cup capacity. Drizzle about ½ teaspoon of the cilantro purée over and serve; set on a warming tray to keep warm, if you wish.

MAKES 8 MINI SOUPS

▲ Double all the soup ingredients (but not the cilantro purée), or serve in smaller portions.

▼ Halve all the ingredients.

☺ Make the cilantro purée and soup up to 1 day ahead, cover, and refrigerate. Thin the soup a bit if needed when reheating.

Celery, Radish, and Parsley Salad with Lemon Dressing

Celery and parsley are two ingredients that don't get the attention they deserve, if you ask me. This bright, crisp, colorful salad is a great example of how well they do at center stage, not just in a supporting role.

LEMON DRESSING

3 tablespoons freshly squeezed lemon juice

Pinch finely grated lemon zest

Salt and freshly ground black pepper

¼ cup olive oil

1 cup thinly sliced radishes (about 1 bunch; halve large radishes before slicing)

1 cup thinly sliced celery, from tender inner stalks

¾ cup lightly packed fresh flat-leaf parsley leaves

To make the dressing, whisk together the lemon juice, lemon zest, and a good pinch each of salt and pepper in a small bowl until the salt is dissolved. Whisk in the olive oil and taste for seasoning, adding more salt or pepper if needed.

Toss together the radishes, celery, and parsley leaves in a large bowl. Drizzle the dressing over and toss to coat the vegetables evenly.

Spoon the salad into 18 porcelain soup spoons and set them on a tray for serving.

MAKES 18 MINI SALADS

▲ Double or triple all the ingredients, serving in other small dishes if you wish.

▼ Halve all the ingredients, or serve larger portions of the salad in larger dishes.

☺ Combine the vegetables up to 2 hours ahead, lay damp paper towels on top, and refrigerate; toss with the dressing just before serving.

THE MIGHTY MANDOLINE

While attending cooking school in France, I was introduced to the traditional French mandoline slicer. It was heavy, durable, and did a mountain of julienning and slicing in no time flat. An indispensable tool in the French kitchen, it was also big, a little clunky, and sometimes hard to use.

I've since fallen in love with the smaller, lighter, and much less expensive Japanese style of mandoline. The one I have includes 3 cutting attachments for varying sizes of julienne strips, and the thickness setting can be adjusted very easily. It's a tool I turn to frequently for making quick, even, and thin slices of firm items such as potatoes, radishes, carrots, and big garlic cloves.

A word of warning: Even those cute little Japanese mandolines mean serious business. I have a small but permanent scar on one finger from a mandoline mishap, though I was helping to prepare a dinner for Julia Child at the time, so I wear it with a tiny bit of pride. There should be a safety guard included in the box—be sure to use it.

Fennel and Corn Salad

This is a delicious example of a salad that holds up well for an evening of grazing and games, which is not the best time to serve a salad of tender greens. Both crunchy fennel bulb and summer's fresh corn have a delicate sweetness to them, partnering beautifully in this simple combination.

2 ears sweet white corn, husks and silk removed

1 medium fennel bulb

2 tablespoons minced fresh chives

1/4 cup olive oil

3 tablespoons white wine vinegar

Salt and freshly ground black pepper

Holding an ear of corn upright on the cutting board, cut downward with a small knife to remove the kernels from the ear, turning it as you go. Repeat with the second ear.

Bring a small saucepan of salted water to a boil and prepare a bowl of ice water. Add the corn to the boiling water and cook for 1 minute. Drain the corn, add it to the ice water, and let cool. Drain the cooled corn and lay it out on paper towels to dry.

Trim the stalks from the fennel bulb, reserving the tender green fronds. Cut the tough base from the bulb, then halve it vertically. Cut out and discard the core, keeping the halves together. Thinly slice the fennel bulb, preferably using a mandoline slicer. Working with 1 small handful of the slices at a time, gather them into a pile and cut them across into 1/2-inch pieces.

Chop enough of the fennel fronds to make 2 tablespoons. Combine the fennel and fronds with the corn and chives in a bowl. Drizzle the oil and vinegar over and toss well to evenly mix. Season to taste with salt and pepper.

Spoon the salad into about 20 porcelain soup spoons or other small dishes, top with a small sprig of any remaining fennel fronds, and set them on a tray for serving.

MAKES ABOUT 20 MINI SALADS

▲ Double or triple all the ingredients.

▼ Halve all the ingredients, or serve larger portions of the salad in larger dishes.

☉ Blanch the corn and prepare the fennel up to 4 hours ahead, top with damp paper towels, and refrigerate. Toss the salad, assemble up to 1 hour ahead, and leave at room temperature.

Baked Clams with Smoked Paprika

This is an easy dish to make, though it does take a bit of time to shell and reassemble the clams for baking. Your payoff will be to see the happy clams you make of your friends!

Choose clams that are at least 1½ to 2 inches across. Before cooking, discard any clams with cracked shells or shells that won't close when tapped; I usually buy a handful extra in case I do need to discard a few.

1½ cups fresh bread crumbs
   (see box, next page)

¼ cup unsalted butter

2 cloves garlic, minced or pressed

36 Manila or other hard-shell clams
   (about 2 pounds), scrubbed

½ cup dry white wine

Rock salt, for baking

2 teaspoons smoked paprika

Preheat the oven to 325°F. Line a rimmed baking sheet with parchment paper or aluminum foil.

Spread the bread crumbs on the baking sheet in an even layer and bake just until dry but not browned, 3 to 5 minutes. Set aside to cool, then transfer the crumbs to a small bowl. Reserve the baking sheet.

Melt the butter in a small saucepan over medium heat, stir in the garlic, and cook gently until aromatic, 1 to 2 minutes. Set aside to cool.

Combine the clams and wine in a large pan, cover, and set over medium-high heat. Shake the pan occasionally and start lifting out the opened clams with a slotted spoon after 3 to 5 minutes. Continue cooking, removing opened clams in batches. Discard any clams that have not opened after 10 minutes. Reserve the cooking liquids in the pan.

When the clams are cool enough to handle, remove the meats and set aside. Separate the shell halves, keeping half of each shell. Rinse the shells and dry on paper towels.

Preheat the oven to 400°F. To help the clams sit steady while roasting, line the baking sheet with ½ inch of the rock salt.

Arrange the cleaned clam shells on the baking sheet, nestling them down into the salt a bit, and add a clam to each shell. Drizzle about ¼ teaspoon of the reserved cooking liquid over each clam.

CONTINUED

BREAD CRUMBS

There's no denying how convenient those canisters of dried bread crumbs are for countless breadings, toppings, and other recipes. But I find them too fine for this recipe. You could shortcut with panko bread crumbs, but keep in mind that they're often lightly sweetened.

Toasting fresh bread crumbs takes just a few more minutes than opening a package, and their almost flaky, more delicate texture is great here. Trim the crusts from 5 or 6 slices of white bread, and cut or tear the bread into pieces. Pulse the pieces in a food processor for a minute or two, until the bread is finely chopped to a crumb texture.

Add the paprika to the bread crumbs and toss. Drizzle the garlic butter over (if solidified, gently warm to melt) and quickly toss to evenly mix. Top each clam with about 1 teaspoon of the crumb mixture, spreading it out a bit.

Bake the clams until the juices bubble at the edges and the crumbs are lightly browned, 3 to 5 minutes. Use tongs to transfer the clams to a serving platter and serve; set on a warming tray to keep warm, if you wish.

MAKES 36 CLAMS

▲ Double all the ingredients, but note that assembly is time consuming.
▼ Halve all the ingredients.
☺ Steam the clams and arrange the clams in the shells on the baking sheet up to 2 hours ahead; cover and refrigerate. Make the crumb mixture up to 2 hours ahead. Assemble and bake just before serving.

Curried Coconut Soup with Shrimp

It's a snap to make a simple shrimp broth with the shrimp shells, which adds an extra dose of flavor to this soup, though you can use light fish stock or water in its place. If the shrimp you're using are larger than 31/35 to the pound, buy an extra 4 ounces or so. The larger the shrimp, the more the 8 used for garnish will take from the soup.

1 pound medium shrimp,
   in their shells

4 cups water

2 tablespoons olive oil

$1/2$ cup finely chopped green onion,
   white and pale green portions

1 tablespoon finely grated or minced
   fresh ginger

2 teaspoons curry powder

$1/8$ to $1/4$ teaspoon dried red
   pepper flakes

Salt

$1 1/2$ cups unsweetened coconut milk
   (reduced fat is fine)

3 tablespoons toasted coconut, for
   serving (optional)

Peel 8 of the shrimp, leaving the tail end of the shell intact. Split lengthwise about half the length of the shrimp, removing the vein; set aside. Fully peel, devein, and finely chop the remaining shrimp. Reserve all of the shells.

Put the shrimp shells in a saucepan and add the water. Bring to a low boil over medium-high heat, reduce the heat to medium-low, and simmer for 15 minutes. Set aside to cool, then strain, discarding the shells.

Heat the olive oil in the same saucepan over medium heat. Add the green onion and ginger and cook, stirring, until tender and aromatic, 2 to 3 minutes. Stir in the curry powder, red pepper flakes, and a good pinch of salt and cook for 1 minute longer, stirring constantly. Add 3 cups of the shrimp broth and simmer gently for 20 minutes. Add the whole shrimp and cook just until opaque through, 1 to 2 minutes. Lift out the shrimp with a slotted spoon and set aside.

Add the coconut milk and chopped shrimp to the soup and cook for about 5 minutes longer. Let cool slightly, then purée with an immersion blender or in batches in a standard blender. Add salt to taste. Reheat over medium-low heat.

Ladle the soup into 8 espresso cups, small heatproof glasses, or ramekins of about $1/2$-cup capacity. Perch a split poached shrimp on the rim of the cup, sprinkle a bit of toasted coconut on the soup, and serve, setting the cups on a warming tray to keep warm, if you like.

MAKES 8 MINI SOUPS

▲ Double all the ingredients.

▼ Hard to halve.

☺ Make up to 1 day ahead, but the soup may become spicier on sitting
   (reduce amount of pepper flakes if you wish); gently reheat before serving.

Masala Crab Salad with Mango

Pappadams, an addictive Indian flatbread made with lentil flour, can be fried or microwaved into the puffed cracker often served at the start of an Indian meal. They accent the rich, sweet crab salad as a wonderful crisp complement. Look for packages of the thin, dry disks in the ethnic foods aisle of your grocery store, or in specialty food stores.

¾ pound crabmeat

1 tablespoon olive oil

¼ cup minced shallot

1½ teaspoons garam masala

⅔ cup finely diced mango

2 tablespoons minced fresh cilantro

2 fried or microwaved pappadams, broken into 16 pieces

Pick over the crabmeat to remove any bits of shell or cartilage. If the crab is rather wet, dry it on paper towels to avoid making the salad soggy.

Heat the olive oil in a medium skillet over medium heat. Add the shallot and cook until tender and aromatic, 1 to 2 minutes. Add the garam masala and cook, stirring, until aromatic and slightly toasty smelling, about 1 minute. Take the pan from the heat and stir in the crabmeat, mango, and cilantro until evenly blended. Let cool, then transfer to a bowl and refrigerate until you are ready to serve.

To serve, spoon the crab salad into 16 porcelain soup spoons and set them on a tray for serving. Top each with a small piece of the crisp pappadam.

MAKES 16 MINI SALADS

▲ Double if you have enough spoons, or serve in other small dishes (with small forks alongside).

▼ Halve all the ingredients, or serve larger portions of the salad in larger dishes.

☺ Make the salad up to 2 hours ahead and refrigerate. Assemble shortly before serving, adding the pappadams at the last minute so they remain crisp.

HAVE DICTIONARY, CAN PLAY

No need to buy a board game for this old standard, which has been the source of homespun fun for many years. It is similar to the general premise of the board game Dictionary Dabble and one of the categories from the bluffing game Balderdash, which is such a popular party game.

Prepare a couple dozen slips of paper. Flip through a dictionary and find some of the most obscure words that you can, writing down one word and its brief definition on each slip of paper. Fold them all and put them in a bowl or hat.

Have paper and pens or pencils for all players. After determining a player to start, he or she will draw one of the words and read the word aloud, keeping the definition secret. Other players will write down the word and a creative / interesting / funny definition for the word. The lead player collects all the definitions and reads them aloud. It's important this person preview all the definitions to make sure they're legible; any hesitation when reading can help give away that it's another player's contribution!

Each player then chooses the definition they feel is the real one. After all player choices are tallied, points are given for the round. Players receive one point each time another player votes for their made-up definition. And players receive two points if they chose the actual definition. Play for a preset amount of time or up to a preset point value, such as fifty.

Mini Shepherd's Pies

Lamb is the traditional meat for a British shepherd's pie, though ground beef is an ideal alternative if you're unable to find (or order) ground lamb. With beef, this technically becomes a "cottage pie" instead. A little trivia for that next round of Foodie Fight.

2 tablespoons olive oil

1 cup finely chopped carrot

1/2 cup finely chopped onion

1 1/2 pounds ground lamb

1/2 cup tomato paste

1/2 cup chopped fresh flat-leaf parsley

1/3 cup dry vermouth or dry white wine

2 teaspoons minced fresh rosemary

Salt and freshly ground black pepper

1 1/2 pounds russet potatoes, peeled and cut in large chunks

1/4 cup half-and-half or whole milk

3 tablespoons unsalted butter

1/2 cup grated sharp cheddar cheese

Preheat the oven to 375°F.

Heat the olive oil in a skillet over medium heat. Add the carrot and onion and cook until the carrot is nearly tender, about 5 minutes. Add the lamb and cook until it is no longer pink, 5 to 7 minutes, breaking up the meat into small pieces as it cooks. Stir in the tomato paste, parsley, vermouth, and rosemary. Season the mixture to taste with salt and pepper and cook a few minutes longer, until well blended and cohesive. Set aside.

Put the potato pieces in a pan of salted water and bring to a low boil over medium-high heat. Reduce the heat to medium and simmer until the potatoes are tender when pierced with the tip of a knife, 10 to 12 minutes. Drain well and let sit for a few minutes, allowing most of the steam to evaporate. Return the potato pieces to the empty pan and mash with a potato masher or large whisk. Add the half-and-half and butter and continue to mash until evenly blended and smooth. Stir in the cheese and season to taste with salt and pepper.

Spoon the lamb mixture into 8 (1/2-cup) ramekins or other small baking dishes. Top with the mashed potato, spreading it evenly. Set the ramekins on a rimmed baking sheet and bake until lightly browned on top and bubbly around the edges, about 25 minutes. Transfer the shepherd's pies to a platter or heatproof tray and let sit 5 to 10 minutes before serving. Serve on a warming tray to keep warm, if you wish.

MAKES 8 MINI PIES

▲ Double if you have enough ramekins, or bake in smaller dishes.
▼ Halve all the ingredients.
☺ Assemble up to 2 hours ahead, cover, and refrigerate; bake shortly before serving.

Kir Royale Floats

This grown-up version of the ice cream float tops homemade cassis sorbet with sparkling wine. Cassis—a liqueur made with black currants that hails from Dijon, France—is the classic ingredient in a kir (when served with white wine) and a kir royale (when the wine is sparkling). This recipe takes me back to a long-ago semester abroad at the University of Dijon; studying the culinary scene was an enchanting extra-curricular activity. Note that you'll need an ice cream maker for the sorbet.

CASSIS SORBET

1½ cups water

¾ cup cassis

½ cup sugar

2 tablespoons freshly squeezed lime juice

1 bottle (750 ml) blanc de blanc sparkling wine

To make the sorbet, combine the water, cassis, and sugar in a small saucepan and bring to a low boil over medium-high heat, stirring to help the sugar dissolve. Reduce the heat to medium and boil for 3 minutes. Transfer the mixture to a heatproof bowl, add the lime juice, and let cool to room temperature. Cover and refrigerate until fully chilled.

When chilled, freeze the sorbet mixture in an ice cream freezer according to the manufacturer's instructions. Transfer the sorbet to an airtight container and freeze until firm but not solid, about 1 hour.

Line a rimmed baking sheet with plastic wrap. Use a small scoop (preferably a spring-type ice cream scoop) to form 2-inch balls of the sorbet and set them on the baking sheet. Freeze until solid, then transfer the cassis sorbet balls to a resealable plastic freezer bag or plastic container.

To serve, put 2 or 3 balls of the cassis sorbet in 8 stemless glasses. Slowly pour the sparkling wine over and serve. The sorbet will melt into the sparkling wine, though your friends may want small spoons to scoop some out in the meantime.

MAKES 8 FLOATS

▲ Double all the ingredients, or triple them if your ice cream maker is large enough.

▼ Serve only as many portions of frozen sorbet balls as needed, saving the rest for another time.

⊙ Make the sorbet up to 2 weeks ahead.

Butterscotch Panna Cotta

Silky panna cotta takes on a butter-and-brown-sugar character in this simple recipe. It makes something of a culinary bluff game; its rich taste suggests an eggy custard, but no eggs are in sight.

1 envelope (2 teaspoons) unflavored gelatin powder

¼ cup cold water

½ cup firmly packed light brown sugar

¼ cup unsalted butter

2 cups half-and-half

3 tablespoons bourbon

1 teaspoon pure vanilla extract

Sprinkle the gelatin powder over the water in a small dish and set aside to soften.

Combine the brown sugar and butter in a small saucepan and cook over medium heat until the butter is melted and the sugar has dissolved, 2 to 3 minutes. Increase the heat to medium-high and continue cooking, stirring constantly, until very smooth, 1 to 2 minutes longer. Take the pan from the heat and carefully whisk in the half-and-half, bourbon, and vanilla extract. If the sugar solidifies at all, warm over medium-low heat to dissolve. While still warm, whisk in the softened gelatin until it is thoroughly melted.

Ladle the mixture into 6 espresso cups or small glasses of about ½-cup capacity and let cool. Cover the cups with plastic wrap and refrigerate until set, at least 3 hours. Uncover the cups and arrange on a platter or tray for serving.

MAKES 6 MINI PANNA COTTAS

▲ Double all the ingredients, or make in smaller glasses for more portions.

▼ Hard to halve.

☉ The panna cotta can be made up to 1 day in advance.

Coconut–Star Anise Rice Pudding

One of the all-time best comfort-food desserts, rice pudding can take on a wonderful array of guises, this one a touch exotic with coconut milk and star anise.

1 (14-ounce) can unsweetened coconut milk (reduced fat is fine)

2 cups half-and-half or whole milk

6 whole star anise

Pinch salt

2/3 cup jasmine rice or other long-grain rice

2 eggs

1/2 cup sugar

2 tablespoons coconut rum or dark rum, or 1 teaspoon pure vanilla extract

1/3 cup toasted coconut

Preheat the oven to 375°F. Generously butter 8 (1/2-cup) ramekins.

Combine the coconut milk, 1 1/2 cups of the half-and-half, star anise, and salt in a saucepan. Bring just to a boil over medium-high heat. Take the pan from the heat and let sit for 1 hour. Return the liquid to a low boil, reduce the heat to medium-low, and stir in the rice. Cook, stirring occasionally, until the rice has absorbed most of the liquid, about 20 minutes. Take the pan from the heat and let cool, stirring occasionally.

In a bowl, whisk the eggs, remaining 1/2 cup of the half-and-half, sugar, and rum until well blended. Stir this into the cooled rice.

Spoon the rice pudding into the ramekins, discarding the star anise as you come across them. Set the ramekins on a rimmed baking sheet and bake until the puddings are set and slightly puffed, about 25 minutes. Let cool slightly, then top each pudding with a sprinkle of the toasted coconut and arrange the ramekins on a serving platter or warming tray to keep warm, if you like.

MAKES 8 MINI RICE PUDDINGS

▲ Double all the ingredients, or bake in smaller dishes for more portions.
▼ Halve all the ingredients.
⊘ Best served shortly after baking, but you can bake it up to 8 hours ahead and refrigerate; warm in a 250°F oven before serving.

7 DRINKS

And what would game night be without some lovely libations? Wine and beer are always welcome, but when you want to treat your guests to a handcrafted cocktail, you have a number of choices here. All these drinks are made to be host-friendly: easy highballs and game-friendly pitcher options so no one needs to be drawn away from the table to shake individual drinks. (The "dummy" from bridge is always a great one to volunteer for such tasks, but most games aren't as accommodating.) I tend to prefer classic drinks; a handful are included in this chapter with subtle adaptations. And I whipped up a few new sippers for you as well. Just the thing to get those creative juices flowing.

Manhattans with Spiced Cherries

Rye whiskey is the original spirit used to make this classic cocktail, one of my favorites in the cooler months of the year. A cousin of bourbon, rye is made with more rye than corn, which gives it a slightly spicy flavor. You can use bourbon instead, if you prefer.

I've always liked my Manhattans "perfect," meaning both dry and sweet vermouths are used, whereas traditionally only sweet vermouth is added. You'll have enough spiced cherries here for a second batch of Manhattans. Note that the cherries need a day to absorb those spicy flavors, so plan ahead.

SPICED CHERRIES

2 cups water

1/2 cup sugar

2 strips orange zest

8 allspice berries

10 whole black peppercorns

4 whole cloves

1 stick cinnamon

16 fresh or frozen sweet cherries, pitted

2 1/2 cups rye whiskey

1/4 cup dry vermouth

1/4 cup sweet vermouth

1/4 teaspoon orange bitters or angostura bitters

To make the spiced cherries, combine the water, sugar, orange zest, allspice, peppercorns, cloves, and cinnamon in a small saucepan. Bring to a boil over medium-high heat, stirring to help the sugar dissolve. Reduce the heat to medium-low and simmer for 20 minutes. Add the cherries and simmer for 1 minute; take the pan from the heat and let cool. Transfer the cherries and spiced syrup to a bowl or jar and refrigerate for at least 1 day before serving.

About 1 hour before serving, combine the rye, dry and sweet vermouths, and bitters in a cocktail pitcher and stir to mix. Refrigerate until you are ready to serve.

Just before serving, add 2 tablespoons of the spiced cherry syrup to the cocktail pitcher along with a handful of ice cubes. Stir to mix well and chill. Put 1 cherry in each glass and pour the Manhattan mix over, leaving the ice cubes behind in the pitcher.

MAKES 8 COCKTAILS

▲ Double or triple all the Manhattan ingredients, refrigerating the extra to refill the pitcher as needed. Double the spiced cherry ingredients to make enough for 4 batches.

▼ Halve all the ingredients.

☺ Make the cherries up to 2 weeks ahead; refrigerate in a well-sealed container. Combine and refrigerate the Manhattan mixture up to 2 hours ahead.

Fresh Greyhounds

Bitters have been gaining an important place in contemporary cocktail culture, with an increase in brands and types available to consumers. Many top bartenders even go so far as to make their own. A little goes a long way in emphasizing flavors in a cocktail, much like salt in a recipe. If you can't find grapefruit bitters (I use the Fee Brothers brand), use other citrus bitters or just omit them.

You'll need about 4 grapefruit to get the amount of juice needed here. The fresh juice really makes a big difference, though you can use good bottled or frozen juice for a short-cut, particularly if you're multiplying the recipe.

2½ cups freshly squeezed pink grapefruit juice

1½ cups vodka

¼ cup simple sugar syrup (page 9)

¼ teaspoon grapefruit bitters (optional)

2 grapefruit slices, quartered, for garnish

Pour enough grapefruit juice into an ice cube tray to make 8 juice cubes and freeze.

About 1 hour before serving, combine the remaining grapefruit juice, vodka, simple syrup, and bitters in a cocktail pitcher, stir to mix, and refrigerate.

To serve, put the juice ice cubes in 8 tumblers or stemless cocktail glasses. Stir the greyhound mixture again and pour it over the ice. Cut a sliver into each grapefruit piece and perch it on the edge of the glasses.

MAKES 8 COCKTAILS

▲ Double or triple all the ingredients, refrigerating any extra to refill the pitcher as needed.

▼ Halve all the ingredients.

☺ Make up to 6 hours in advance and refrigerate.

Rosemary Martinis

I'm pretty much a purist when it comes to martinis. I can't bring myself to imagine what's involved with Martini: The Game, a cards-and-dice game that makes each player a bartender working to whip up cocktail creations. My version of that game would be pretty boring: a bunch of gin cards, the occasional dry vermouth card, and a die that just says "olive" or "twist" on all sides. Not a fun game, but these ingredients do make a superior cocktail in my opinion!

So I'm not big on martini variations, but this one minor twist on the classic martini simply adds a bit more herbal and savory character to the aromatics already present in the gin—a little more depth of character without going overboard. This cocktail will be best with a London dry–style gin. Some newer and small-batch gins—much as I love them—can have distinctive character that may or may not meld well with the rosemary. To ensure that the olives take on some of that savory rosemary flavor, they should soak for at least a day before mixing the martinis.

16 pimento-stuffed olives, in brine

1 tablespoon chopped fresh rosemary

1 (6-inch) sprig fresh rosemary

1 bottle (750 ml) gin

¼ cup dry vermouth

At least 1 day before serving, combine the olives and chopped rosemary in a small dish and pour over some of the brine from the olive jar to cover. Cover and refrigerate.

About 1 hour before serving, rub the sprig of rosemary between the palms of your hands for 10 to 15 seconds and put it in a cocktail pitcher. Pour the gin and vermouth over, stir to mix, and refrigerate.

Just before serving, add a generous handful of ice cubes to the pitcher and stir gently for a minute to give it an extra dose of chill. Pour the martini into stemless martini glasses, leaving the ice behind in the pitcher. Very briefly rinse the olives to remove any clinging rosemary and spear 2 each onto cocktail picks or small rosemary sprigs (with lower leaves removed), adding a pick to each glass.

MAKES 8 COCKTAILS

▲ Double or triple all the ingredients, refrigerating extra to refill the pitcher as needed.

▼ Halve all the ingredients.

☺ Marinate the olives up to 1 week ahead (be sure they're covered in brine) and refrigerate. Prepare the gin and vermouth with rosemary and refrigerate up to 2 hours ahead.

Lava Lounge Punch

This is the punch I concocted to help christen the Lava Lounge party room in the basement of our classic 1956 ranch house. I painted the walls tangerine orange and the floors a deep blue. There are lots of twinkling lights across the ceiling, a vintage lava lamp in one corner, and a large rattan chair in another. With a growing assortment of island memorabilia—much of it donated by friends—this has turned into one outstanding party and game room, complete with pool table and turntable for the vinyl collection.

For this punch, I love the exotic tang of passion fruit juice. Try to find a juice as close to "pure" as possible, not too sweet or with added flavorings. You can use mango juice in its place.

2 cups orange juice, preferably freshly squeezed

1 cup pineapple juice

¾ cup passion fruit juice

½ cup freshly squeezed lime juice

1½ cups dark rum

¼ cup Chambord or other berry liqueur

Stir together the orange, pineapple, passion fruit, and lime juices in a pitcher. Pour enough of the juice mixture into an ice cube tray to make 8 juice cubes and freeze. Add the rum and Chambord to the remaining juice mixture and refrigerate until you are ready to serve.

To serve, put the juice ice cubes in 8 tumblers. Stir the punch to mix and pour it over.

MAKES 8 PUNCH COCKTAILS

▲ Double or triple all the ingredients, refrigerating extra to refill the pitcher as needed.

▼ Halve all the ingredients.

☺ Mix up to 6 hours ahead and refrigerate.

DICE IS NICE

Various versions of this game have been played in many parts of the world for many generations. Sometimes called farkle, keepers, 10,000, and a number of other names, I've always known it as zilch. And I have always played it with the same green dice from the little metal tin that once held the fruit-flavored "bon bon drops" that my mother so loved. A scrap of paper in her handwriting is nestled beneath the dice. Rules vary a bit game to game. Here's how we played it.

Everyone rolls one die; the player with the highest number goes first.

The player rolls six dice at once. At least one point-valued die or combination of dice (noted below) must be rolled for the turn to continue. The player sets aside at least one of the point-valued dice from the roll and has the option of standing with those points, or rolling the remaining dice to gain more points.

As before, at least one of the dice from this new roll must have point value; with fewer dice to roll comes greater risk that no points will be earned on a roll. Any roll for which there are no points earned is a "zilch," and all points accumulated for that turn are lost.

When a player has successfully rolled to achieve point values on all six dice, he or she can pick up all the dice (after noting the total points) and continue rolling to further collect points.

To first get on the scoreboard, a player must earn at least 500 points in one turn. For future turns there is no minimum point value needed. Play continues clockwise to other players. The game ends when the first player reaches a predetermined point value. We usually played to 10,000.

Point values (all must be from a single roll):

one 5	50 points	three 6s	600 points
one 1	100 points	three 1s	1000 points
three 2s	200 points	three pairs	2000 points
three 3s	300 points	1, 2, 3, 4, 5, 6	3000 points
three 4s	400 points	six 1s	10,000 points
three 5s	500 points		(a game-winning roll!)

Strawberry-Ginger Champagne Cocktails

There's a beautiful blush to this cocktail from the addition of the freshly made strawberry-ginger syrup to cheery sparkling wine—the kind of blush you might take on when you hear some of the more risqué answers your friends come up with for a round of Say Anything. The gentle sweetness of the syrup makes it an ideal complement to a dry style of sparkling wine, such as a blanc de blanc.

¾ cup water

⅓ cup sugar

⅓ cup coarsely chopped fresh ginger

1 cup chopped fresh or frozen strawberries

1 (750 ml) bottle blanc de blanc sparkling wine

6 strawberry slices, for garnish

Combine the water and sugar in a small saucepan and bring to a low boil over medium-high heat, stirring to help the sugar dissolve. Add the ginger and simmer over medium heat until aromatic, about 5 minutes. Stir in the strawberries and set aside to macerate for at least 1 hour.

Strain the syrup through a fine sieve, pressing gently on the ginger and berries to extract a maximum of flavorful liquid without pressing solids through. Cover and refrigerate until needed.

To serve, spoon 2 tablespoons of the strawberry-ginger syrup into 6 stemless wine glasses or small tumblers and pour the sparkling wine over. Make a vertical cut in the strawberry slices and perch them on the edges of the glasses before serving.

MAKES 6 COCKTAILS

▲ Double or triple all the ingredients.

▼ Use as much syrup as needed, refrigerating extra for a few days to serve another time.

☺ The syrup can macerate for up to 4 hours. The strained syrup can be refrigerated for up to 3 days. Mix the cocktails just before serving.

Bloody Marys with Fresh Horseradish

The Bloody Mary often suffers from its own universal appeal, so common that many renditions are, well, common. This one is different, with a couple of touches that include using freshly grated horseradish and making fresh celery juice (easy!) to lighten the tomato juice a bit.

If you're unable to find fresh horseradish root to grate yourself, you can use bottled. By far my favorite garnish for this drink is pickled asparagus spears. If you're unable to find them, you can use a simple stick of celery instead. And if you have a juicer, certainly use that for the celery juice, though the food processor technique is pretty quick.

3 cups coarsely chopped celery

3 cups tomato juice

1½ cups vodka (regular or pepper)

¼ cup freshly squeezed lemon juice

1 tablespoon freshly grated horseradish

1 teaspoon Worcestershire sauce

½ teaspoon Tabasco sauce

¼ teaspoon celery seeds

Salt

10 spears pickled asparagus

Process the celery to a pulp in a food processor. Scoop the pulp into a fine-mesh sieve set in a bowl and press on it with a spatula to draw off as much celery juice as you can. You should have about ¾ cup juice.

Stir together the celery juice and tomato juice in a pitcher. Pour enough juice into an ice cube tray to make 10 juice cubes and freeze. Stir the vodka, lemon juice, horseradish, Worcestershire sauce, Tabasco, and celery seeds into the remaining juice. Season to taste with salt (the tomato juice may already be rather salty) and refrigerate until it is needed.

Just before serving, put 1 juice ice cube in each tumbler and add a couple of regular ice cubes. Stir the bloody Mary mixture and pour it over the ice. Add a spear of pickled asparagus and serve.

MAKES 10 COCKTAILS

▲ Double or triple all the ingredients, refrigerating the extra to refill the pitcher as needed.

▼ Halve all the ingredients.

☺ The flavors are best if made not more than 4 hours in advance.

Pomegranate-Mint Fizz

So you didn't make a mint at The Game of Life and retire to Millionaire Estates? No worries, you can get a dose of the green stuff here. Refreshing, colorful, and quick to make, this cocktail has easy-breezy flavors that all your guests will love.

3 cups pure pomegranate juice

¼ cup loosely packed mint leaves

1 cup currant vodka or other berry vodka

¾ cup plain seltzer or sparkling water

¼ cup simple sugar syrup (page 9)

Mint sprigs, for garnish

About 1 hour before serving, pour the pomegranate juice into a cocktail pitcher. Rub the mint leaves between the palms of your hands for a few seconds and add them to the juice. Stir to mix and refrigerate.

Just before serving, add the vodka, seltzer, and simple syrup to the pitcher and stir to mix. Half-fill 8 tumblers with ice, pour the fizz over (through a small sieve to hold back the mint leaves, if desired), and garnish with mint sprigs.

MAKES 8 COCKTAILS

▲ Double or triple all the ingredients, refrigerating the extra to the refill pitcher as needed.

▼ Halve all the ingredients.

☺ Combine the pomegranate juice and mint up to 4 hours ahead; finish just before serving.

Key Lime Gimlet Cocktails

Little Key limes seem to be traveling more these days. I'm able to buy good-sized bags of them at my neighborhood grocery store for just a few dollars. And they're good for a lot more than just pie. The slightly more complex flavor makes for a particularly bright addition to a gimlet, though you can use regular Persian limes instead.

8 thin slices Key lime or halved slices regular lime

2 cups gin

½ cup freshly squeezed Key lime juice or regular lime juice

⅓ cup simple sugar syrup (page 9), plus more to taste

¾ cup plain seltzer or sparkling water

Put the lime slices in 8 ice cube tray sections, fill with water, and freeze.

About 1 hour before serving, combine the gin, lime juice, and simple syrup in a cocktail pitcher. Stir to mix and refrigerate.

Just before serving, stir the seltzer into the gin mixture. Put the ice cubes in 8 small tumblers or stemless cocktail glasses and pour the gimlets over.

MAKES 8 COCKTAILS

▲ Double or triple all the ingredients, refrigerating the extra to refill the pitcher as needed.

▼ Halve all the ingredients.

☺ Combine the ingredients up to 6 hours ahead, adding the seltzer just before serving.

GASTRO GAMES: GOURMETSMARTS ET AL
(SmartsCo, 2002)

This family of flash card–style trivia games allows you to choose the degree of competition you're up for. Each themed set—Gourmet, Beer, Cocktail, Wine, Coffee, Chocolate—has four categories of trivia cards. For instance, in the CocktailSmarts game they're "Ingredients," "Drinks," "Lingo," and "Wild Card." Cards are shuffled, answers are given, and scores are tallied. If your competitive spirit is plum tuckered out, just quiz each other more informally and marvel at your collective mental acuity. Or make a house rule that clever, funny answers deserve some points, too.

Orange Negronis

The classic negroni is a cocktail with roots in Italy. High on the list of amazing cocktail experiences I've had is sipping a negroni (or was it two?) in the cocktail enclave of Harry's Bar in Venice. Traditionally, the recipe is equal parts Campari, sweet vermouth, and gin. I temper the bitterness by dropping the Campari a bit, and add just-squeezed orange juice for a dose of fresh flavor.

1 cup sweet vermouth
¾ cup freshly squeezed orange juice
¾ cup Campari
1½ cups gin
Orange zest twists, for garnish

Stir together the vermouth, orange juice, and Campari in a cocktail pitcher. Pour enough of the mixture into an ice cube tray to make 8 cubes and freeze. Add the gin to the remaining vermouth mixture and refrigerate until you are ready to serve.

Put the vermouth-mixture ice cubes (they likely won't be rock solid because of the alcohol content, but that's fine) into 8 stemless cocktail glasses or tumblers, and pour the negronis over. Add an orange zest twist to each and serve.

MAKES 8 COCKTAILS

▲ Double or triple all the ingredients, refrigerating extra to refill the pitcher as needed.
▼ Halve all the ingredients.
☺ Make up to 6 hours in advance and refrigerate.

Watermelon-Rosé Sangria

Sangria takes on a lot of different personalities using different wines—traditional red, white, or even rosé—and varying the complementary fruit added to the wine. I'm a big fan of the dry, elegant rosés of summertime, which make a wonderful foundation for refreshing, beautiful sangria.

3½ cups fresh watermelon juice (see box)

1 (750 ml) bottle dry rosé wine

¼ cup brandy

½ orange, halved and cut across into ¼-inch slices

1 lime, halved and cut across into ¼-inch slices

8 (1-inch) cubes watermelon, for serving

Pour 1½ cups of the watermelon juice into an ice cube tray and freeze.

Combine the remaining juice with the wine, brandy, orange slices, and lime slices in a large pitcher, stir to mix, and refrigerate for at least 1 hour.

To serve, put the watermelon ice cubes in 8 stemless wine glasses or tumblers. Stir the sangria and pour it over the ice cubes, adding a slice or two of the orange and lime to each glass. Skewer the watermelon cubes at the end of small skewers or long cocktail picks and add them to the glasses.

MAKES 8 SANGRIAS

▲ Double or triple all the ingredients, refrigerating the extra to refill the pitcher as needed.

▼ Halve all the ingredients.

☺ Assemble the sangria up to 8 hours ahead and refrigerate.

WATERMELON JUICE

If you have a juicer, make the juice according to manufacturer's instructions. If not, it's easy to make nonetheless.

For the amount of juice needed in this recipe, start with about 7 cups of coarsely chopped watermelon (roughly half of a small round watermelon). Remove all the seeds you can find. Purée the melon in batches in a food processor or blender until quite juicy, then pour it into a fine sieve set over a bowl and let sit to drain. You can stir the pulp a bit to help drain off the juice, but don't press on the pulp so the juice will remain as clear as possible.

Mocha Almond Java

As the evening ebbs and it's time for a little coffee, consider offering your guests this version spiked with spirits of the coffee-chocolate-almond variety. This is a great partner for the Walnut Sablés with Maple-Walnut Cream on page 84.

½ cup whipping cream

2 tablespoons powdered sugar

3 cups freshly brewed strong coffee (regular or decaf)

½ cup Godiva or other chocolate liqueur

½ cup Disaronno amaretto or other nut liqueur

¼ cup Kahlua or other coffee liqueur

Whip the cream until slightly thickened, add the powdered sugar, and continue whipping until soft peaks form. Refrigerate until you are ready to serve.

Combine the coffee and liqueurs in a 1-liter thermos carafe, seal well, and gently turn the carafe to mix the ingredients. Pour the coffee into coffee cups, top each with a generous dollop of the whipped cream, and serve.

MAKES 6 COFFEES

▲ Double if you have 2 carafes, or make in batches.

▼ Halve all the ingredients.

☺ Make up to 2 hours ahead if your carafe holds heat very well.

It's not hard to get your hands on a Scrabble board, the latest edition of Cranium, or one of the newer specialty versions of Monopoly. But when you want to expand your game-night horizons and learn more about the increasingly popular European imports, modern strategy games, and other game options outside the mainstream, hit an independent neighborhood game store like these below. While talking with these games merchants, I found that popular sellers across the country include Settlers of Catan, Ticket to Ride, Pandemic, Dominion, Bananagrams, Say Anything, and Apples to Apples. And you can still pick up Balderdash and some Magic: The Gathering cards for your nephew while you're at it.

Most, if not all, of these game stores offer these amenities: board game and other themed game nights for drop-in play, sample games on hand to try before you buy, hundreds of games to choose from (if not a thousand or more), and supremely knowledgeable staff who can help steer you to just the right game for your collection. They all stock a broad range of games, from classics and party games for the casual game player to specialty and collectable games for the hard-core game enthusiast.

This is just a sampling. If you have a favorite game store not on this list, let me know about it at **www.gourmetgamenight.com**. And should you be unable to find a game store in your area, many of these stores offer online sales as well.

ALL FUN & GAMES
958 US Highway 64
Apex, North Carolina 27523
919-468-6322
www.allfunngames.com
Year established: 1999

BLUE HIGHWAY GAMES
2203 Queen Anne Avenue North
Seattle, Washington 98109
206-282-0540
bluehighwaygames.com
Year established: 2007

CRITICAL HIT GAMES
89 Second Street
Coralville, Iowa 52241
319-338-4263
www.criticalhitgames.net
Year established: 2005

GAME NIGHT GAMES
2030 South 900 East, Suite E
Salt Lake City, Utah 84105
801-467-2400
www.gamenightgames.com
Year established: 2004

GAMEDAZE
Multiple locations
Phoenix area and Tucson, Arizona
800-396-8511
www.gamedaze.com
Year established: 1994

GAMES OF BERKELEY
2151 Shattuck Avenue
Berkeley, California 94704
510-540-7822
www.gamesofberkeley.com
Year established: 1980

GREAT HALL OF GAMES
5501 North Lamar Boulevard
Austin, Texas 78751
512-505-0055
www.greathallgames.com
Year established: 2000

MYRIAD GAMES
8 Stiles Road
Salem, New Hampshire 03079
888-869-7423
www.myriadgames.com
Year established: 1999

RAINY DAY GAMES
18105 SW Tualatin Valley Highway
Aloha, Oregon 97006
www.rainy-day-games.com
503-642-4100
Year established: 1998

THE FAMILY GAME STORE
Historic Savage Mill
8600 Foundry Street
Savage, Maryland 20763
888-776-5980
familygamestore.net
Year established: 2005

THE GAME PRESERVE
Multiple locations
Indiana
www.gamepreserve.com
800-414-2637
Year established: 1980

THE GAMES PEOPLE PLAY
1100 Massachusetts Avenue
Cambridge, Massachusetts 02138
888-492-0711
www.thegamespeopleplaycambridge.com
Year established: 1974

A

Aged Cheddar with Dried Cherry-Almond Chutney, 55
Alfredo's Food Fight (Fundex Games), 87
All-Edibles
    Aged Cheddar with Dried Cherry-Almond Chutney, 55
    Artichoke-Stuffed Mushrooms, 56
    Baby Baja Tacos, 65
    Cinnamon Meringues with Chocolate Mousse, 73
    Herbed Biscuits with Smoked Salmon, 59
    Meringues with Fresh Berry Filling, 69
    Mini Tostadas with Cumin Black Beans, 57
    Mocha Cheesecake Bars, 72
    Orange Tuile Cones with Cassata Filling, 70–71
    Polenta Squares with Spicy Sausage and Spinach,
        62–63
    Roasted Red Potatoes with Bacon-Chive Crème
        Fraîche, 68
    Salmon Poke in Endive Leaves, 60
    Shrimp Cakes in Shiso Leaves, 66–67
    Stuffed Large Pasta Shells with Kale-Ricotta Filling, 64
    Tuna Tartare on Daikon Slices, 58
Artichoke-Stuffed Mushrooms, 56
Avocado Soup with Roasted Poblano Cream, Chilled, 112

B

Baby Baja Tacos, 65
Baked Clams with Smoked Paprika, 119–20
Banana
    Banana Bread with Hazelnut-Cream Cheese Filling, 91
    Nutella and Banana Galettes, 106

Beef
    Beef Empanadas with Black Beans and Jalapeño,
        100–101
    Beef Yakitori, 50
    Mole Flank Steak with Pickled Peppers, 52
    Peppered Steak with Balsamic Red Onions, 49
    Spicy Meatballs with Yogurt-Cucumber Dip, 46–47
Biscuits, Herbed with Smoked Salmon, 59
Bloody Marys with Fresh Horseradish, 137
Blue Cheese Dip, 24
Blue Highway Games, 4, 144
BoardGameGeek.com, 101
Bread crumbs, 120
Broth, vegetable, 113
Brown Butter Pound Cake with Caramel Dip, 34–35
Butterscotch Panna Cotta, 127

C

Caesar Dip with Big Croutons and Romaine, 18
Capers, fried, 21
Cassis Sorbet, 126
Celebrity Chef! The Game (Idea Farm NYC), 33
Celery, Radish, and Parsley Salad with Lemon Dressing,
    116
Cheesecake, Mocha Cheesecake Bars, 72
Chicken
    Chicken Salad Sandwiches with Orange and Walnuts,
        77
    Crostini with Chicken Liver Mousse and Kumquats, 29
    Empanadas with Chicken and Walnuts, 103–4
    Poached Chicken Breast, 77

Chilled Avocado Soup with Roasted Poblano Cream, 112

Chocolate

    Chocolate Tartlets with Brandy Cream, 105

    Cinnamon Meringues with Chocolate Mousse, 73

    Mocha Almond Java, 143

    Mocha Cheesecake Bars, 72

    Mole Flank Steak with Pickled Peppers, 52

    Personal Chocolate-Port Fondues, 36

Chutney, 55, 81

Cinnamon Meringues with Chocolate Mousse, 73

Clams with Smoked Paprika, Baked, 119–20

Coconut, 121, 128

Coffee

    Mocha Almond Java, 143

    Mocha Cheesecake Bars, 72

Cookies, 70–71, 84–85

Cooking techniques, basic, 8–9

Corn and Fennel Salad, 118

Corn, Sage Popcorn, 111

Crackers, Olive and Cheese, 97

Crostini with Chicken Liver Mousse and Kumquats, 29

Crostini with Wild Mushroom Tapenade, 20–21

Cumin Spiced Nuts, 110

Curried Coconut Soup with Shrimp, 121

D

Dice Is Nice, 135

Dips and spreads

    Blue Cheese Dip, 24

    Brown Butter Pound Cake with Caramel Dip, 34–35

    Caesar Dip with Big Croutons and Romaine, 18

    Crostini with Chicken Liver Mousse and Kumquats, 29

    Crostini with Wild Mushroom Tapenade, 20–21

    Edamame Purée in Cherry Tomatoes, 19

    Green Goddess Dip, 24

    Green Pea and Mint Spread with Crispy Pancetta, 30

    Homemade Pretzel Sticks with Three Mustards, 27–28

    Individual Cheese Fondues with Apples and Ham, 32

    Oven-Baked Potato Chips with Onion Dip, 22–23

    Personal Chocolate-Port Fondues, 36

    Radishes with a Trio of Dips, 24–25

    Romesco Dip, 25

    Spicy Meatballs with Yogurt-Cucumber Dip, 46–47

Dough, 95–96, 106

Dried Cherry-Almond Chutney, 55

Drinks

    Bloody Marys with Fresh Horseradish, 137

    Fresh Greyhounds, 131

    Key Lime Gimlet Cocktails, 140

    Lava Lounge Punch, 134

    Manhattans with Spiced Cherries, 130

    Mocha Almond Java, 143

    Orange Negronis, 141

    Pomegranate-Mint Fizz, 138

    Rosemary Martinis, 132

    Strawberry-Ginger Champagne Cocktails, 136

    Watermelon-Rosé Sangria, 142

E

Edamame Purée in Cherry Tomatoes, 19

F

Fennel, 45, 98–99, 118

Fish. *See* Seafood

Fondue, 32, 36

Fondue pots, mini, 33

Foodie Fight (Chronicle Books), 23

Food Lover's Trivia (We3Chefs.com), 71

Fresh Greyhounds, 131

Fried Capers, as garnish, 21

G

Games

    about, 1–5

    Alfredo's Food Fight, 87

    Celebrity Chef! The Game, 33

    Dice is Nice, 135

    Foodie Fight, 23

    Food Lover's Trivia, 71

    Gourmet Smarts et al, 140

    Green Eggs and Ham Speedy Diner Game, 87

    Have Dictionary, Can Play game, 123

    Score Four game, 46

    Slamwich, 87

    Wasabi! 58

Games magazine, 47

Game stores, 144–45
Garlic, roasting, 8–9
Ginger juice, 58
Ginger-Strawberry Champagne Cocktails, 136
Glasses and cups, 7–8
Gourmetgamenight.com, 144
Gourmet Smarts et al (SmartsCo), 140
Green Eggs and Ham Speedy Diner Game (I Can Do
    That Games), 87
Green Gazpacho, 114
Green Goddess Dip, 24
Green Pea and Mint Spread with Crispy Pancetta, 30
Grilled Garlicky Mushrooms, 40

H
Have Dictionary, Can Play game, 123
Herbed Biscuits with Smoked Salmon, 59
Herb-Marinated Shrimp, 43
Homemade Pretzel Sticks with Three Mustards, 27–28

I
Ice Cream Sandwiches, 89–90
Individual Cheese Fondues with Apples and
    Ham, 32
Itty Bitty BLTs, 78

K
Key Lime Gimlet Cocktails, 140
Kir Royale Floats, 126

L
Lamb
    Lamb and Olive Kebabs, 48
    Lamb Burgers with Feta, 83
    Mini Shepherd's Pies, 124
Lava Lounge Punch, 134
Lentil and Carrot Soup with Cilantro Purée, 115

M
Mandoline slicer, 116
Manhattans with Spiced Cherries, 130
Marinade, Teriyaki, 50
Masala Crab Salad with Mango, 122

Menu planning, 11–15
Meringues
    Cinnamon Meringues with Chocolate Mousse, 73
    Meringues with Fresh Berry Filling, 69
Mini Shepherd's Pies, 124
Mini Tostadas with Cumin Black Beans, 57
Mint, 30, 138
Mocha Almond Java, 143
Mocha Cheesecake Bars, 72
Mole Flank Steak with Pickled Peppers, 52
Mousse, 29, 73
Mushrooms, 20–21, 40, 56, 102
Mustard, Homemade Pretzel Sticks with, 27

N
Nuts
    Banana Bread with Hazelnut-Cream Cheese Filling, 91
    Chicken Salad Sandwiches with Orange and Walnuts,
        77
    Cumin Spiced Nuts, 110
    Dried Cherry-Almond Chutney, 55
    Empanadas with Chicken and Walnuts, 103–4
    Mocha Almond Java, 143
    Nutella and Banana Galettes, 106
    PB&J Blondie Bites, 86–87
    toasting, 9
    Walnut Sablés with Maple-Walnut Cream, 84–85

O
Orange Negronis, 141
Orange Tuile Cones with Cassata Filling, 70–71
Oven-Baked Potato Chips with Onion Dip, 22–23

P
Panna Cotta, Butterscotch, 127
Pasta, Stuffed with Kale-Ricotta Filling, 64
Pastries
    Almost Bite-Sized Pizzas, 95–96
    Beef Empanadas with Black Beans and Jalapeño,
        100–101
    Chocolate Tartlets with Brandy Cream, 105
    Empanadas with Chicken and Walnuts, 103–4
    Mushroom and Goat Cheese Tartlets, 102

Nutella and Banana Galettes, 106
Olive and Cheese Crackers, 97
Raspberry and Cream Cheese Turnovers, 108
Roasted Fennel Focaccia with Pecorino, 98–99
PB&J Blondie Bites, 86–87
Peppered Steak with Balsamic Red Onions, 49
Personal Chocolate-Port Fondues, 36
Petits Croque Monsieurs, 76
Pickled Grape and Blue Cheese Skewers, 39
Pickled peppers, 80
Pies, Mini Shepherd's, 124
Pimento Cheese Tower Sandwiches, 80
Pizza, Almost Bite-Sized, 95–96
Poached Chicken Breast, 77
Polenta Squares with Spicy Sausage and Spinach,
    62–63
Pomegranate-Mint Fizz, 138
Popcorn, Sage, 111
Pork
    Green Pea and Mint Spread with Crispy Pancetta, 30
    Individual Cheese Fondues with Apples and Ham, 32
    Itty Bitty BLTs, 78
    Petits Croque Monsieurs, 76
    Polenta Squares with Spicy Sausage and Spinach,
        62–63
    Pork Saltimbocca, 42
    Pork Tenderloin with Rhubarb Chutney, 81
    Roasted Red Potatoes with Bacon-Chive Crème
        Fraîche, 68
    Spicy Meatballs with Yogurt-Cucumber Dip, 46–47
    Stuffed Large Pasta Shells with Kale-Ricotta Filling, 64
Potatoes
    Oven-Baked Potato Chips with Onion Dip, 22–23
    Roasted Red Potatoes with Bacon-Chive Crème
        Fraîche, 68
Pretzels, Homemade with Three Mustards, 27–28
Pudding, Coconut-Star Anise Rice, 128
Puréeing, 8–9

R
Radishes, 24–25, 116
Ramekins and/or bowls, 7
Raspberry and Cream Cheese Turnovers, 108

Recipes
    about, 5–6
    menus, 11–15
    serving pieces, 7–8
    serving tips, 10–11
    shortcuts, 6
Rhubarb Chutney, Pork Tenderloin with, 81
Roasted Red Potatoes with Bacon-Chive Crème Fraîche,
    68
Romesco Dip, 25
Rosemary Martinis, 132

S
Sage Popcorn, 111
Salads
    Celery, Radish, and Parsley Salad with Lemon
        Dressing, 116
    Chicken Salad Sandwiches with Orange and Walnuts,
        77
    Fennel and Corn Salad, 118
    Masala Crab Salad with Mango, 122
Salmon
    Herbed Biscuits with Smoked Salmon, 59
    Salmon Poke in Endive Leaves, 60
Sandwiches
    Banana Bread with Hazelnut-Cream Cheese Filling, 91
    Chicken Salad Sandwiches with Orange and Walnuts,
        77
    Ice Cream Sandwiches, 89–90
    Itty Bitty BLTs, 78
    Lamb Burgers with Feta, 83
    PB&J Blondie Bites, 86–87
    Petits Croque Monsieurs, 76
    Pimento Cheese Tower Sandwiches, 80
    Pork Tenderloin with Rhubarb Chutney, 81
    Walnut Sablés with Maple-Walnut Cream, 84–85
Score Four game, 46
Seafood
    Baby Baja Tacos, 65
    Baked Clams with Smoked Paprika, 119–20
    Curried Coconut Soup with Shrimp, 121
    Herbed Biscuits with Smoked Salmon, 59
    Herb-Marinated Shrimp, 43

Seafood, *continued*
 Masala Crab Salad with Mango, 122
 Salmon Poke in Endive Leaves, 60
 Shrimp Cakes in Shiso Leaves, 66–67
 Swordfish and Fennel Skewers, 45
 Tuna Tartare on Daikon Slices, 58
 Wasabi Pea-Crusted Tuna, 41
Serving pieces, 7–8
Serving tips, 10–11
Shortcuts, cooking, 6
Shrimp
 Curried Coconut Soup with Shrimp, 121
 Herb-Marinated Shrimp, 43
 Shrimp Cakes in Shiso Leaves, 66–67
Silicone baking mats, 70
Simple sugar syrup, making, 9
Skewers and picks
 about, 8
 Beef Yakitori, 50
 Grilled Garlicky Mushrooms, 40
 Herb-Marinated Shrimp, 43
 Lamb and Olive Kebabs, 48
 Mole Flank Steak with Pickled Peppers, 52
 Peppered Steak with Balsamic Red Onions, 49
 Pickled Grape and Blue Cheese Skewers, 39
 Pork Saltimbocca, 42
 soaking, 48
 Spicy Meatballs with Yogurt-Cucumber Dip, 46–47
 Swordfish and Fennel Skewers, 45
 Wasabi Pea-Crusted Tuna, 41
Slamwich (Gamewright), 87
Small Dishes
 Baked Clams with Smoked Paprika, 119–20
 Butterscotch Panna Cotta, 127
 Celery, Radish, and Parsley Salad with Lemon
  Dressing, 116
 Chilled Avocado Soup with Roasted Poblano Cream,
  112
 Coconut-Star Anise Rice Pudding, 128
 Cumin Spiced Nuts, 110
 Curried Coconut Soup with Shrimp, 121
 Fennel and Corn Salad, 118
 Green Gazpacho, 114

Kir Royale Floats, 126
Lentil and Carrot Soup with Cilantro Purée, 115
Masala Crab Salad with Mango, 122
Mini Shepherd's Pies, 124
Sage Popcorn, 111
Soup
 Chilled Avocado Soup with Roasted Poblano Cream,
  112
 Curried Coconut Soup with Shrimp, 121
 Green Gazpacho, 114
 Lentil and Carrot Soup with Cilantro Purée, 115
 Vegetable Broth, 113
Spicy Meatballs with Yogurt-Cucumber Dip, 46–47
Spoons and forks, 8
Spreads. *See* Dips and spreads
Strawberry-Ginger Champagne Cocktails, 136
Stuffed Large Pasta Shells with Kale-Ricotta Filling, 64
Sugar syrup, making, 9
Supplies, essential, 7–8
Sweet Pastry Dough, 106
Swordfish and Fennel Skewers, 45

T

Tacos, Baby Baja, 65
Teriyaki Marinade, 50
Tomato Sauce, 95
Tostadas with Cumin Black Beans, 57
Tuna Tartare on Daikon Slices, 58

V

Vegetable Broth, 113

W

Walnut Sablés with Maple-Walnut Cream, 84–85
Wasabi Pea-Crusted Tuna, 41
Wasabi! (Z-Man Games), 58
Watermelon juice, 142
Watermelon-Rosé Sangria, 142

Y

Yogurt-Cucumber Dip, Spicy Meatballs with, 46–47